THE HIP

Ivory Joe Hunter

THE HIP

Hipsters, Jazz and the Beat Generation

by

Roy Carr   Brian Case   Fred Dellar

faber and faber

LONDON · BOSTON

First published in 1986 by
Faber and Faber Limited
3 Queen Square London WC1N 3AU
Printed in Great Britain by
W.S. Cowells
Ipswich Suffolk

This one's for
Eugene and Paolo
and
Ronnie and Pete

© *Roy Carr, Fred Dellar and Brian Case (The Three*
Must Get Theirs for Original Illustrated Record
Productions), 1986

DESIGN BY ANDY MARTIN/STUDIO ESPRESSO

Front Cover Photo: Chet Baker 1953 by Bob Willoughby
Back Cover Photo: Dexter Gordon

British Library Cataloguing in Publication Data

The Hip.
  1. Arts, Modern — 20th century
  I. Carr, Roy
  700'.9'04   NX456

ISBN 0-571-13809-8

*If you're talking about what's hip, then this is the hippiest
list anyone's put together. Know 'em all. Either worked with
'em or lived with 'em. And, anyone that even gets around to
telling how Babs Gonzales would hustle his book at every
cat's funeral really knows the score. Let me tell you this,
when you go into any club to hear some music, you can tell
immediately who's hip — they're the ones who ain't talking
when someone's on stage playing.*

— Slim Gaillard (June 1986)

CONTENTS

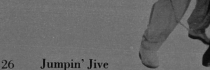

GENUINE
UNBORN CALF

INTRO...

HIP is hard to nail. It no more responds to definition than it does to the common light of day, which is little. It can't be taught. Hip suspects words and manifestos, and has not developed a recruitment pitch since it doesn't recruit. The hipster always assumes that the membership is filled, even when – particularly when – he is the only cat on the case. Hip is an understated state of grace that does not necessarily wish the world well. Hip is self-sufficiency, Jack.

HIP lives along the rising smoke from a cigarette parked under the rods of a Selmer Mark VI during the saxophone solo, rides a fingersnap on the off-beat, claps only triplets. It hints at its presence in the rake of a hat and the wristy dismissal. Hip has a great ear and a great eye and a greater instinct, but is easy-over on the words. It communicates with itself. Hip has shifted more shades than any other philosophy throughout history, but fewer manuals and no pyjama cases.

HIP has never been about hippies, nor majorities and fashions, freaks and first-withs, the flounderers after a star to steer by. It is sometimes present in the pool shark and almost always absent in the pop star, here and not there, and its subtle signs and signals are infinitely reverberating...

HIP is an uncrackable code for good reason. It was devised to defend the cat's quick kernel from the rip-off. Many of its patron saints died of that, burned out, soul-sick, self-contemptuous, and fumbling with the boredom in the back of the neck which comes from watching commerce's cold clones overtake. Rip-off can be fatal. Lester Young, the hipster's hipster, laid this shortly before he faced the final wall: 'A lot of the ladies are playing *me* and making the money.'

HIP has rewired the nervous system to accommodate the overload of ecstasy and to coast through the cut-out of exhaustion, registering upon the dial only the immobile needle of a hang-loose ironic cool. Hip lays low, lives in the margin and twists and tumbles to a driving adrenalin panic within, while hoisting an off-peak impassivity for the square world without. Repeat: without.

The hipster first entered the language in the early fifties, a concept copped from blacks by whites, along with the music. The hipster was born with bebop. Both were war babies, and while the rest of the nation was piling its hair in a munition worker's bang on the brow and were shoulder-padding to the big bland strains of Glenn Miller – the khaki mixing promiscuously on a pass with the utility underwear and whistling 'Happiness Is Just a Guy Called Joe' – bebop and hip were hopping down the clubs along 52nd Street in New York and Central Avenue, LA. In the decade of Digging For Victory, they were plain digging, period.

Some comics and some actors have got some of the moves together since then, and sired a dynasty. There's a direct line from Lord Buckley through Lenny Bruce to Richard Pryor and Eddie Murphy, and from Marlon Brando to Robert De Niro. Chroniclers of the hipster life begin with The Beats and beat on in the lyrics of Tom Waits. Dime paperback thriller writers got it right more often than Hollywood; movies and jazz, America's contribution to this century's art forms, have seldom been successfully combined.

This book is intended as a bouquet to HIP...some scenes, some sayings, some sounds. It would be Ivy Jivey to attempt more.

THREADS, TREADERS
AND
THE RIGHTEOUS RIM

PYTHON KNOB
Style 2422 — Amazing, new, super-simulated Python skin shoe. Made in combinations of coppertone Python with brown patent leather; black and white Python with black patent leather.
Now ONLY $13.95
plus postage

THE MISTER B FLEX-ROLL COLLAR

Billy Eckstine 'People ask me, "B — why don't you put 'em out again?" I've still got a bunch of 'em, use 'em for golf now mainly. That shirt was created because when I was blowing trumpet and trombone with the Earl Hines band, my neck swelled. If I put on a conventional shirt to blow, I popped the buttons on it. I got the idea of putting the collar band only half-way — no collar band at the sides so you could stick your hands down in there and it'd still look neat.

'I never thought the thing'd catch on. I wore one of them in that picture with Esther Williams, *Skirts Ahoy* — and my God, everybody's saying, B! — man, that shirt!

'So I thought, Ah, gooooood! I made a deal and gave the pattern to The Sea Island Shirt Company in Georgia, and they put 'em out. Then I had my own shop that a buddy of mine, Bobby Redcross, was running. You know that song Bird did, "Red Cross"? He named it after him.

'Eddie "Lockjaw" Davis still wears 'em, and he's always after me for the original pattern. I say, no way, baby. See, the ones Jaws wears, he has to pull 'em up at the back. You don't have to pull 'em up. There's a secret to that. The coat pulls 'em up. Well, that shirt, it's the old expression, necessity being the mother of invention. I mainly did it to keep from popping buttons.'

THE GERRY MULLIGAN HAIRCUT

Gerry Mulligan 'It didn't start out as a crew-cut. I often had bad luck with barbers. I'd go in a shop and come out with a new personality. "Oh, a crew-cut? Zip!" I'd look like a defrocked monk. I try to stay away from them. I used to cut it short myself, and it lay forward. My reason for doing that was that by the time I was eighteen or nineteen, my hairline was receding. I realized that the act of training my hair back, which my mother had done when I was a kid – you know, they used that guck to glue it down – was breaking the hairs off. I thought, to hell with it, cut all my hair off and brushed it forward. Ha! – what an interesting thing to realize my hair grows forward, not back! I may have influenced a lot of musicians because I was very much proselytizing the idea that you can save your hair by combing it in its natural direction. Follow the energy patterns that the hair expresses, and you'll hang on to it longer.'

BABS AND THE JAZZ BOW TIE

Babs Gonzales 'In the middle fifties Alan Freed was the boss of New York disc jockeys. I had known him from Cleveland when he was on a small station there in 1952. He was very close to the Birdland people but he still was cool with me. Me and a girl named Lorenzo Shihab had made us a new bow tie. It was the size of a king-sized cigarette, cloth over a piece of wood. In a month all the musicians and down people were wearing it. Alan hit on me to let him manufacture it. The only drag is, he didn't want to give us but eight cents a tie. It sold for a dollar and only cost ten cents to make. I asked for a quarter a tie. He had the power of radio and if he had sold 400,000, I wanted some of the bread. We never came to terms but Lorenzo and I sold about a thousand anyway.'

THE BERET

Dizzy Gillespie 'Perhaps I remembered France and I started wearing the beret. But I used it as headgear I could stuff into my pocket and keep moving. I used to lose my hat a lot. I liked to wear a hat like most guys then and the hats I kept losing cost five dollars apiece. At a few recording sessions when I couldn't lay my hands on a mute, I covered the bell of the trumpet with the beret. Since I'd been designated their *leader*, cats just picked up on the style.'

NB: Dizzy became such a sartorial celebrity that, after being photographed with his trouser-fly accidentally undone, overnight scene-makers coast-to-coast could be viewed proudly sporting front-ventilated strides!

'We herewith submit a preview of men's Easter fashions from the world's least inhibited fashion centre, Harlem. Trousers will be deeply pleated, with waistband just under the armpits, 30-inch knees, and 15-inch cuffs. A popular suit jacket is one that measures 36 inches down the back seam and has a fly front, shoulders padded out 3½ inches on each side, two breast pockets, and slashed side pockets. This may be worn with a white doeskin waistcoat. Shoes are pointed, the most popular leathers being light-tan calfskin and coloured suede. Hats may be worn in the porkpie shape or with crowns 6 inches high. Colours, as always, are limited only by spectrum.'

The New Yorker (1941)

THE LAST OF THE FAT PANTS

August Darnell alias Kid Creole 'Ever since I was a small boy, my father would always dress me up in two or three piece suits and put a *chapeau* on my head.

'That love of attire grew into a search for the clothes that made my idols look the way they did – so I looked frantically for the kind of look that Humphrey Bogart or John Garfield had. I noticed that the trousers were free falling and that the jackets were boxed back . . . their hats, but especially the material.

'Whenever I went to a tailor and asked them about lowering the crotch and making the pants bigger they'd all look at me as though I was a reject from 1940. They couldn't comprehend what I was saying. It wasn't until 1974 when my brother found this original antique pair of slacks – 1940 gaberdine baggies – that the search ended. When I put them on, I said, "Ah! this is what's been missing all the time." It was magic. A very relaxed feel which enabled me to assume a much closer position to my idols.'

'Miles Davis, the world's most famous trumpet virtuoso, will be a resplendent sight at the Brooklyn Paramount. He will wear an especially designed jazz suit made in Italy of special light weight material, as soft as cashmere, but as strong as some of the notes Miles plays. He will display a cutaway jacket, with new 6-inch wide trousers.'

A press statement to herald the appearance of Miles Davis at the week-long Randall Island Jazz Festival, staged in Brooklyn during October 1959.

LESTER LEAPS IN

Lester Young's first recorded solo on 'Shoe Shine Boy' sent shockwaves through the jazz world of 1936. Nobody had heard a tenor sax sound like that before! Up until Lester leaped in, Coleman Hawkins had dominated the instrument with his big bold bulldozer attack. Lester was coming from somewhere else. Holding the horn at an awkward vaudeville musician's angle, he came bumping like a snake through the canebrake. His tone was light and buoyant, and his solos powered along without melodrama. He played hopscotch with bar lines and beat, his phrases bounding joyously forward or easing by with a sly, sinuous sidle. It is, perhaps, the first musical portrait of the hipster.

He was an original away from the horn too. He made up his own language, some of which remains current jazz slang. A fastidious dresser, Lester's trademark was the famous flat-topped porkpie hat. An intensely private, solitary man, he presented a cool, unruffled blank to most of the world – except when he played. It is said that the only way you could tell when he was upset was when he reached into his top pocket for a little whisk broom to dust off his shoulder.

Billie Holiday nicknamed him Pres – The President – and he gave her the title Lady Day. Musically, they were made for each other. His work with the Count Basie band and his own small combos established a style that you can still hear in the playing of tenormen everywhere, from Dexter Gordon to Stan Getz, and Zoot Sims to Warne Marsh.

Art Blakey 'Pres was invited to the White House to meet President Truman. He didn't like Truman, but he didn't stand up and say nothing, you know, run off his mouth. When

Lester and Lady

they said, "Mr President, we want you to meet the President of the Saxophone", the President came over and stuck out his hand to shake hands. Pres backed away, shook his head and said, "Nicely, nicely."

'One time when Pres was going out the studio door, Poppa Jo Jones said, "What time do we go back on?" So Pres looked at his watch, and said, "A deuce of bells a ding-dong."'

Lester Young—Volume 5

Evening of a Basie-ite

PREZ

Buddy Tate 'I was with Victoria Spivey's Revue. She'd just made the first black picture, *Hallelujah*, for King Vidor. We were in a hotel in Tulsa, Oklahoma, best hotel in the world at that time for blacks, I believe. Owner was an oil magnate, and he had a Steinway in the lobby and everybody'd go in there and jam.

'We were down there one morning, jammin', high, having a good time, when somebody said to me there was a tenor player upstairs, Red Young. I went up. He was lying in his room, three or four corn pads on his toes. I woke him up. I says, we're having a session downstairs, why don't you come along and play because I haven't heard you play tenor. I'll never forget that sound! Light, very light, but aaah! Everybody put their horns down on the floor and left. He scared everybody to death! That was in the early thirties.'

Buddy Tate 'We were together in the Basie band, did a little tour and we came to New York. I'll never forget that. I was standing at the station, country boy in a big long overcoat and a big hat, just stickin' out, you know. Everybody else was grabbing cabs. I didn't know where to go. But Pres had waited for me. "I'm gonna take you with me up to the Woodside Hotel. All the ladies want to see their pound cakes." He referred to their wives as their pound cakes, see.

'A lotta musicians beat the Draft by saying, "Well – I didn't get it, I was on the road." We were all trying to stay out because we were making too much money and there were so many lonely ladies. We were playing three months in Watts, Los Angeles, and this young guy came out one night. Zoot suit on, big chain down to the knees like Cab Calloway, introduced himself. We thought he was a fan. He stayed all night. He said, "I'd like for you and Lester and Sweets and Jo to be my guests" – and he bought drinks and drinks and drinks. At the end, he pulls this badge and shows it to Lester and Jo Jones. "Be at this address at 9 o'clock in the morning or we'll come and get you and you'll go to jail for five years." It upset Lester. He said, "Goddamn it – ain't that a bitch! The little guy – I liked him! He gained my confidence. I started to turn him on!" I said not to worry, because by this time Lester's drinking a quart of 100 per cent proof a day, and they won't want Jo either because he's crazy. But, man – the next day they put them in the Army.

'The last time I saw Pres, I shared a car journey with him

back to New York. When I got in, he opened up. "Now, let's review the books, Lady Tate. A lot of the ladies are playing me and making the money." See, he never felt he'd had the recognition he should've had.'

Above: *Pres, Ronnie and Flip*
Below: *Pres and Friend*

Ronnie Scott 'Lester took me into his dressing-room. He'd got this beer stein with a lid, full of joints. He said to me "Eyes?" When I lit one up, he said "Bells?"'

Billy Eckstine 'We had this little midget, Pee Wee Marquette, the emcee at Birdland, on tour with us. We were on the bus, and he kept stepping over Pres while Pres is shooting dice. "Lemme get out, Pres." So finally Pres says, "Will you SIT DOWN, you half a muthafucker!"'

Gil Evans 'Pres could hardly stand to talk in any ordinary way. The way people talk was just too hackneyed for him, and he always had to do something else. He'd walk on the bandstand at Birdland like a parakeet, right – I don't know why – and he'd say to the band, "The Water on the Front". He meant "I Cover The Waterfront", but he couldn't stand to say it.'

Art Blakey 'He had to see his thing stolen from him, and everybody make money. He wasn't making it. He told me he didn't expect to live past fifty. Since it's like it is, he can't make a living and he can't even feed himself, it's better for him to go on and split. And that's what he did.'

Gil Evans 'He was determined he wanted to die, but he didn't want to kill himself. He wanted to die in an extended way, which he did. Took a year to do it. He came back to the Alvin Hotel right across from Birdland for the last year of his life, leaving his wife out in Long Island. He wanted to spend his time in the old way in a sense, surrounded with musicians. He had a great big room in the hotel, and all around the room on every little place where you could set it was food that people had brought to him. But he hardly ate. Only drank wine. For a while I was trying to get him to eat, but all of a sudden the whole picture dawned on me. I saw exactly what he was doing, so I gave up. We had fun instead because there's no point in trying to talk someone out of destiny.

'Even when he was in this tragic condition he was funny. I mean – phew! His wife was pregnant so I said, "Pres – when's the baby coming?" He said, "Oh, those people'll be here in December." That tickled me.

'Now, although he was in that kinda condition, he needed a haircut, so my wife was very good at cutting hair, so we came over. She takes a comb and scissors and starts cutting. Pres says, "Lemme see it! Lemme see it!" Every little piece from then on that she cut off he had to see it because he wanted to be just so. Here's a man who is on his way out and he knows it and all that, but on his way out he wants to have the hair be right. Sweet man.'

McVOUTY

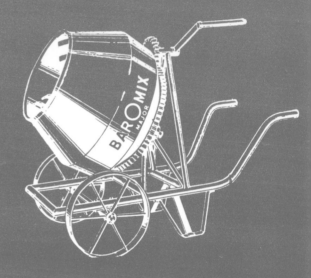

Now Dean [Moriarty] approached him, he approached his God: he thought Slim [Gaillard] was God: he shuffled and bowed in front of him and asked him to join us.

'Right-orooni', says Slim; he'll join anybody but won't guarantee to be there with you in spirit. Dean got a table, bought drinks, and sat stiffly in front of Slim. Slim dreamed over his head. Every time Slim said, 'Orooni,' Dean said, 'Yes!'

I sat there with these two madmen. Nothing happened. To Slim Gaillard the whole world was just one big orooni.

extract from On The Road *by Jack Kerouac*

Tall, bearded under the beret, soft-spoken and infinitely spaced in delivery, Bulee 'Slim' Gaillard was date-stamped by the bebop forties and it never wore off.

'French fries-o-rooni', he tells the waitress in a purring zonked voice, 'and leave the eyes open on the eggs.'

That whole o-rooni backslang started life in Slim's stage act, and swept the nation's hipsters in the war years. A favoured form of greeting being:

'How was the Vout?'

'Oh very o-rooni.'

'Hey! Macskooto!'

Slim's nonsense songs, in which he was partnered first by Slam Stewart (Slim 'n' Slam) and then by Bam Brown (Slim 'n' Bam), were pretty much improvised in the moment in clubs and even in recording studios. 'Cement Mixer' emerged fully grown by happenstance: a cement mixer was in use outside the studios; Slim, taking five, watched it for a moment, then ran back inside and commemorated it in song. It charted immediately, and so did 'Flat Foot Floogie', which joined 'The Stars And Stripes' in a time capsule at the World's Fair.

Slim's career really took off after that. He secured a Wednesday residency on Frank Sinatra's weekly CBS radio show, got a part in the zany Hollywood movie, *Hellzapoppin'*, and would have been in *Stormy Weather* but for the call-up, which had him flying B-25s. Jamming with Thelonious Monk and Charlie Christian at Minton's, waxing with Bird and Diz, and organizing bebop beanos at Birdland – Slim was the man of the moment, in the right place at the right time. Clubs formed about him. He ran his own Spanish food restaurant (he loves to cook) which sold his own Vout City Beer. He held a long-running residency at Hollywood's famous Billy Berg's Club where he frequently upstaged visiting celebrities and from which he peddled his legendary Vout Dictionary for just a quarter.

His jive jargon enjoyed enormous vogue. Bob Hope asked Marlene Dietrich what she thought of Slim Gaillard on his radio show. 'Vout!' she replied.

Most of Hollywood dug Slim. His good looks, personality and striking wardrobe put him in the big league as a date, pulling screen goddesses like Ava Gardner, Lana Turner and Rita Hayworth. Yards of gossip about him – 'They called me Dark Gable', he chuckles – were written by Hedda Hopper, Louella Parsons and Walter Winchell.

He was both a regular house guest at the Howard Hughes mansion and a person of impulsive style.

Slim Gaillard's most notorious escapade began when he hailed a cab outside San Francisco's Say When Club and instructed the driver to take him to the Oasis Club as quickly as possible.

'Where's that?' enquired the cabbie.

'On Western Avenue.'

'Where's that?'

'In LA.'

'*That*'s different', exclaimed the driver gunning the gas.

Slim, who was headlining with Lionel Hampton, was due on the stand at 9 pm. Arriving at the Oasis with less than three minutes to spare, Slim dashed past the anxious club

David Stone Martin's cover design for Slim's Opera in Vout

19

manager, asking him to take care of the cab.

'How much?' enquired the club owner reaching for his wallet.

'Two fifty', said the cabbie checking his meter.

The clubowner handed over three dollars adding, 'Keep the change.'

'Uh-huh', retorted the exhausted cabbie. 'Two *hundred* and fifty.'

The story made coast-to-coast headlines.

'Yeah!' Slim chuckles softly at the memory, and then recalls a few of his legendary contemporaries.

LEO WATSON

'Scatting! Leo was the creator – things like "Nagasaki"...the best. When we worked The Radio Room in Hollywood, the place was always full of stars, so he'd sit at his drums and see who was at the tables and start singing in rhythm, "Hey! a-look-a-there, here comes Betty Grable ...ta-pitti-ta-vouti-de-boo-boom-ketting-ting...look out! I see Bette Davis and hey, look at ol' Clark Gable, ker-boom-boom." He'd riff, he'd jive, he'd sing about things like Hippopotamus lips!'

HARRY 'THE HIPSTER' GIBSON

'Harry and I worked together a lot – used to sing a lot of my tunes, but then he started doin' his own things like "Who Put The Benzedrine In Mrs Murphy's Ovaltine" and tell the audience to get Benzedrine inhalers and put them in their Coca Cola, saying "You get h-i-g-h!"

'Eventually, he got busted and his songs banned.

'I remember, I had a two-week engagement in San Bernardino and Harry – who was finishing up a spell in jail – was to join me for the second week. Well, he got them to put a big sign outside the club which announced, "Opening Friday Night. Direct From San Quentin Prison – Harry 'The Hipster'."'

JACK KEROUAC

'Having Jack write about me in *On The Road* is a nice thing to have on your report card.

'He was a great listener...really admired my work ...When I played The Say When Club in San Francisco, Jack showed up every night...would stand with his back against the wall and while he listened all the girls would cruise by and admire him. Between sets, I'd stand there right next to him. We were both so sharp we made a Gillette blade look like a hammer.

'There was one girl – owned two-thirds of Palm Springs – who'd keep telling me, "Slim, you're the most fantastic guy I've ever seen!" Anyway, I wasn't about to argue...Then, one night when I came to the club, there was a key on the piano with my name on it. She'd gone out and bought me a brand new car as a little token...hey! It's good to be handsome!'

He laughed, wiped up the remains of the eggs with a bread roll, and chased it all down with a bottle of Perrier.

SO, WHAT EVER HAPPENED TO...

BAM BROWN?

'You gotta know your own limits. Unfortunately, Bam wasn't that cool. Pot couldn't satisfy him, so he tried everything else that was going, but even that didn't seem to be of any use.

'It was when we were in the bar in a big St Louis Hotel (with Lena Horne) that Bam suddenly dashed off the stage into the kitchen only to return with a big long knife. Then, he told the audience, "I'm gonna cut everyone of you up into little pieces!" He'd completely flipped out. Eventually, they got him in a strait-jacket and took him to hospital where he remained for the next eight years. They let him out once, but he almost killed his mother, so they put him back in again, where he remained until he died.'

LEO WATSON?

'Another one who didn't know his own limits...just went downhill...stayed plastered all day and all night ...couldn't seem to drink enough wine. It was tragic, in the end, he was sleeping on the Bowery sidewalks. Leo Watson ...guess he was the kind of person nobody could help.'

HARRY 'THE HIPSTER' GIBSON?

'He and his piano live happily together in a trailer somewhere in Florida where he grows all his own vegetables and putti-putti!'

There are only two men that I look up to ...
Slim Gaillard and Dizzy Gillespie. Without them
I wouldn't be playing.

– Miles Davis

Slim's charm had him a regular on San Diego's 'Sun Up' (KFMB-TV) where he and a rookie weather-girl frequently hung-out at the track. Fired from her job, she did somewhat better as Raquel Welch. Slim featured in John Cassavetes' *Too Late Blues* and guested on prime time's *Marcus Welby MD* and *Roots*, as well as contributing to *Midnight Love* – the last album proper by his son-in-law, Marvin Gaye.

A jazz festival attraction, today, Slim also enjoys youth-cult status in England. But then, Slim has always been a source of wonderment to the young.

Stan Getz, still in short pants, would pester Slim to be allowed to jam at one of his Sunday afternoon sessions. Parental approval was given on conditions. The sharp-suited Slim Gaillard, tightly holding little Stan's hand as he walked the youngster home and delivered him safely, became a familiar double-take for seen-it-all eyes.

21

THE BEBOP BABBLERS

Above: *The Original Spirit of Rhythm Leo Watson*
Right: *Joe "Be Bop" Carroll and Dizzy Gillespie*

Scat-singing, the wordless vocal that imitates the blowing instrumental solo, may have started with Louis Armstrong who dropped his lyric sheet during the recording of 'Heebie Jeebies', but the bebop forties raised the art to lunacy. It was like the only way a cat could join in with those spiky, supercharged hundred-bar-a-minute themes was by striking his knees together like flints – and babbling.

'Be-y'abba-dah-ool-ya
Be-y'abba-dah-ool-ya-koo'

Bebop anthems like 'Oo-Bop-She-Bam', 'Oo-Shoo-Be-Doo-Be', 'Oop-Bop-A-Da' and 'Ool-Ya-Koo' were the scattergun vowel howls that burst out from somewhere between the beret and the goatee all along the 52nd Street clubs. Scat is a jumping cracker.

Singers like Eddie Jefferson, Slim Gaillard, Leo Wat-

son, Babs Gonzales, Joe Carroll and Eddie 'Pancho' Hagood were the precursors of today's rap raconteurs. There is little street difference between Gonzales' brand of expubidence or Gaillard's vouteroonie and the hippity-hop quick mix of Grandmaster Flash and Kurtis Blow. It has been the hipster's vernacular for four decades.

There have been the usual generation-gap hassles, however. When Dizzy Gillespie's 1947 RCA waxing of 'Oop-Bop-A-Da' moved 700,000 seventy-eights, a sour Satchmo reworked the innocent glee-club glucose of 'The Whippenpoof Song' into the acid 'The Boppenpoof Song'. This gassed nobody. The disc was withdrawn two days after release in Britain.

Scat wasn't easy to sing, though it sounded it. Billy Eckstine, who discovered the seventeen-year-old Sarah

Diz

Vaughan at an Apollo talent contest – and no mean scat-cat himself – says this: 'You've gotta have a knowledge of what you're gonna do. I think that's what's wrong with the imitators. They start to run a change and all of a sudden they've painted themselves into a corner. If you don't know what the chords are, you don't know how to come back on out of it. A lot of these chicks, man, start one of those real deep things, that Sass does, from what they hear Sass does. Well, that *ain't* the way Sass'd do it. Some of them'll finish with a nice big breath – and leave the rest of their change hanging up in the ceiling somewhere.'

The Royal Family of scat were Sarah Vaughan, Ella Fitzgerald, Betty Carter, Leo Watson and Mel Torme. Below that were Clown Prince Slim Gaillard and, down the bottom of the tree, Court Jester Babs Gonzales. Babs could've been a maniac if he could've settled down. Between writing memoirs on the run (*I Paid My Dues – Good Times No Bread* and *Movin' On Down De Line*), running his own New York niterie (Babs' Insane Asylum), singing with his band (Three Bips and A Bop), selling his own record label (Expubidence

Publishing Corporation) out of a battered suitcase, he chauffeured (chauffeur show good) for the rakish Errol Flynn.

'I had been on my gig three months and one day Errol Flynn hit on me to work for him as a chauffeur. He explained I wouldn't have to wear the monkey suit, etc., and could stay sharp. Naturally I accepted and started with him. All I had to do was drive him to work in the morning, pick him up and take him home in the evening. That way I had the car all to myself from nine-to-four every day. I would just cruise Hollywood Boulevard and pick up pretty little chicks. I had to cop white, Chinese or Hawaiian girls, as I was passing for an Indian, turban and all.'

Babs was the original jive-ass hustler, even barking his wares at a friend's funeral. He was never too shy to ask for a free flop for his Bips and A Bop. 'I cut into her saying, "Baby, since four of us got to grease everyday, why not let us cop the food and you do the burnin."'

Who first beeped the bop is open to argument. White singer and one-time GI paratrooper Dave Lambert (later to

Above: *The Three Bips and a Bop*
with Babs Gonzales (extreme left)
Left: *Eddie Jefferson*

score with Lambert-Hendricks-Ross) is reputed to have cut the first scat bop anthem, 'What's This?', with the Gene Krupa Band. But the legend was Leo Watson. 'WAIT! Leo Watson! LEO WATSON was in a class by HIMSELF!' says Mel Torme. 'Ella, Sarah, myself – we're all jazz-influenced, jazz-oriented singers – but Leo Watson was the FIRST and ONLY guy who really was a jazz singer. Listen to him on Gene Krupa's "Nagasaki". That's what scat singing is all about, not "Scoobie Ba-Da-Bum". The truth is that scat singing is the toughest kinda singing. I'm talking about how your mouth is stretched outa shape; I'm talking about taking a specific chord pattern and, with never knowing what you're gonna sing at that moment, to indeed sing.'

Scat rides again today in the jet-assisted Bobby McFerrin, and, if you get him on the right night, in the gymnastic Al Jarreau. Scat is impossible to separate from vocalese, which is singers putting words to classic instrumental solos. Eddie

Jefferson, recently murdered by a shotgun blast from a moving car as he took the night air outside a club, was probably the founder. He always claimed that he and Bird doped it out together round a piano. Clarence Beeks, better known as King Pleasure, grabbed Jefferson's version of 'Moody's Mood For Love' (a vocal version of James Moody's solo on 'I'm In The Mood For Love') and got it out there on wax ('There I go, there I go, there I go, pretty baby, you are the soul who snaps my control'). And it still sells today. George Benson's cover version went platinum. Similarly, both Chaka Khan and Manhattan Transfer have taped 'A Night In Tunisia' with Dizzy Gillespie guesting.

British expatriate Annie Ross wrote words to tenorman Wardell Gray's 'Twisted' way back when, and decades later Joni Mitchell recorded her try. Annie Ross was part of the most ambitious attempt ever to let the singers blow, teaming with Jon Hendricks and Dave Lambert, and taking Basie's most famous arrangements and solo breaks for a whole album entitled *Sing A Song Of Basie*. Multi-dubbing caught the feel of sixteen men swingin'.

25

JUMPIN' JIVE

Hamp and House

The summer of 1942: Lionel Hampton is *the* hottest thing in black music, having formed a trail-blazing seventeen-piece outfit that simply tears audiences apart.

The saxes honk and scream, the trumpets – according to reliable eye-witnesses – *breathe* smoke and the rhythm section rocks so hard that ballroom bobbysoxers and their beaux are forced to jitterbug and jive, in a most unholy fashion, until exhaustion piles them in untidy heaps upon the maple floor.

While the world at large is engaged in war, across the States, Harlem and Kaycee jump music blasts out from relatively new-fangled machines called jukeboxes. Meanwhile, somewhere along the Potomac River a brightly coloured pleasure boat floats.

On board, frenzied vibraphone star and warlord Lionel Hampton can be found goading his most celebrated side-man, Illinois Jacquet – the toughest of tenormen – through the umpteenth chorus of his current smash, 'Flying Home', and the passengers into mass hysteria.

Suddenly, a sweat-soaked Hamp spins around, trans-fixes his bassist Vernon Alley with a wild-eyed stare and screams, 'Hit the water, Gate!' So caught up in the euphoria is his obedient sideman, that Alley promptly tosses aside his double bass and dives, fully clothed, off the deck and into the drink.

Jump music can have this effect . . .

Inspired by star-crossed Texas guitarist and fellow Benny Goodman cohort, Charlie Christian, Hampton assembles the wildest-ever big band, stocked with the fiercest young turks of the day. More than once, anxious

theatre-owners call in surveyors to check out a building's foundations halfway through one of Hamp's flag-waving stampedes, when it seems as though enough energy is being generated to run the entire New York subway.

Musically, Hamp's is the blackest and most undisciplined gang in town and, as such, never attains the society endorsement afforded the more urbane bands of The Duke and The Count.

Should an alarmed theatre manager drop the curtain in an effort to cool off the overheated Hampton, it has the reverse result. Both Hamp and his henchmen just crawl under the crushed-velvet to carry on their rumpus in the front row of the stalls.

One year later: having successfully beaten out the likes of Ellington and Basie to win *Metronome* magazine's coveted Top Band award, Hamp flies down to Kansas City to participate in a 'Battle Of The Bands' showdown. A box-office sell-out is predicted.

The seers are right. By the time Hamp arrives, some 14,000 perspiring young cats are jammed into the city's auditorium.

Hamp – he turns it all on. Pounds the drums, jiggles his sticks, plays speed-of-light vibes, indulges in his two-fingered pianistics, hoofs hard and fast and yells 'Hey! Ba-Ba-Re-Bop' encouragement as the band rabble-rouses in back.

With no room to dance, the kids simply stand and yell back, waiting for the inevitable finale – 'Flying Home', Hamp's killer-diller. . . a no-prisoners-taken assault on a riff, which leaves all rival bands with no moves to make, except turn and run.

As the hysteria abates, on ambles Louis Jordan – a musical good-humour man – short, dapper and ready-to-please. As his little combo takes its place on the stand, Jordan beams at the house, winks knowingly and begins to sing.

'I tell you baby, we're gonna move away from here.

I don't want no iceman lookin' in my Frigidaire,

That's why we're gonna mo-oo-ve to the outskirts of town.'

Then, when Jordan blows his first choruses on his well-travelled alto sax, Hamp can't believe what is happening.

'He just played the blues', he later complains. 'Louis, with just piano, bass and drums, just playing the blues. And, he cut my ass. He really cut my ass!'

Top: *Illinois* Middle: *Jaws* Bottom: *Bullmoose*

It's been called a lotta things over the years. Right now we're dealing with that exciting era when it cavorts under the title of Jump Music.

The style first raised its honkin' head around the close of the glamorous thirties: a riff-rife small combo off-shoot of big bands, capitalizing on a recent boogie-woogie explosion.

As jump's mainman, Louis Jordan affirms: 'With my little band, I did everything they did with a big band. I made the blues jump.'

That he did.

Jump is hot-spot hedonism. Its main characteristics: breakneck tempos fast enough to outdistance the roadrunner; more self-mocking humour than a season of *Bilko* re-runs; and lyrics so hip they're almost surreal – as in 'Plant ya now, an' dig you later!'

It's the decade of flashing grins and neon ties, dominated by zoot-suited, conk-haired battling tenor sax men who honk, scream and squeal into their golden horns whilst 'walking the bar' – the saxman's equivalent of Chuck Berry's 'duck walk'.

The sheer excitement these wild men generate is best illustrated by the audacious antics of 'Deacon's Hop' hit-hipster, Big Jay McNeely. Not only is Big Jay prone to one hour solos, ripping off his jacket and writhing around the floor on his back prior to bar walking, he is also notorious coast-to-coast for parading through ape-shit crazy audiences and out into Main Street where he out-honks passing traffic.

When, in Beaumont, Texas, Big Jay decides to extend his *walk* as far as the neighbourhood slammer, the local sheriff promptly invites him in and throws away the key. Meanwhile, Big Jay's sidemen are still on stage, righteously riffing in anticipation of their boss retracing his steps. When he doesn't return on cue, they dash down to the jailhouse and spring him in order to avoid a full-scale riot. The same thing happens in San Diego.

Big Jay McNeely is yet another jump jiver who publicly cuts the ass of the mighty Lionel Hampton. The location: Wrighley Field baseball stadium. Hamp is playing host to 30,000 disciples. It takes but one number of Big Jay's set before Hamp's wife (Gladys) drags the saxman off to prevent him winning the day. However, as Hamp takes the band for a front-of-stage walkabout, Big Jay runs on to the field, past third base and reaches the stands, where he begins to blow, to the crowd's delight.

'Hamp's wife was mad', says Big Jay, 'but there was nuthin' she could do. I was up in the audience and all the kids were hollerin' and screamin' for me, the hometown boy. I marched all the way around the stadium. Hamp wasn't gonna be outdone. He took the whole band off-stage and marched right around the stadium to where home plate is. When I saw that, I started crawling on my back from second base all through the dugouts. And he still had to follow me . . . we all ended up in the dugouts.'

At the Golden Gate Drive-In in LA, Big Jay raced around on roller-skates, wearing a cast-off toga from Ben Hur. He was arrested for 'exciting Mexicans'.

It's usually easy to name the most popular practitioners in any major trend, but in this instance pinpointing precisely where the joint first jumped is trickier than Alex Haley's search for his *Roots*.

What we do know is that the non-refined big bands headed by leaders like Lucius 'Lucky' Millinder, Jay 'Hootie' McShann, Chick Webb, Hot Lips Page, Andy Kirk, Erskine Hawkins and Milt Larkins, not to mention Walter Page's legendary Blue Devils (the latter destined to become the Count Basie Orchestra), were proving grounds for the future scene-setters.

It was from the ranks of such outfits – most of whom frequently roamed the south-west states – that screamers and shouters such as hornmen Buster Smith, Charlie Parker (Bird was a bluesman to the end), Earl Bostic, 'Bullmoose' Jackson, Illinois Jacquet, Arnett Cobb, Jack McVea, the be-turbanned Lynn Hope, Tab Smith, Hal 'Cornbread' Singer, Sam 'The Man' Taylor, Red Prysock, Big Al Sears, Eddie 'Lockjaw' Davis, Sonny Stitt, Eddie 'Cleanhead' Vinson, Joe Houston and Johnny Griffin, organist Bill Doggett, and singers Wynonie 'Mr Blues' Harris and Walter Brown first sprang.

Among the closely-linked aspects of jumpin' jive are the 'Hi-De-Ho' showbiz shenanigans of the sartorially slick Cab Calloway – self-proclaimed Dean of Jive – and the nonsensical McVoutie hipster patois of famed 'Flat-Foot Floogie' protagonist Slim Gaillard.

The one common denominator is the concern with letting good times roll. The recurring themes of deprivation and good love gone bad that previously formed the core of urban blues take a back seat. Jump is party time. It preaches optimism, self-respect and the prospect of more.

Arguably, Louis Jordan is the first of many to sing black and proud. So what if your big-legged mama has flown the coop? A well-dressed honeydripper can always find young chicks to fry.

Cab Calloway and Louis Jordan stand as jump's main-men. Indeed, without their remarkable back-catalogue, a devoted fan like Joe Jackson would have found it impossible to piece together his 1981 *Jumpin' Jive* tribute, and the Chevalier Brothers wouldn't have a career.

Calloway is the first superdude. Author of the *Hipster's Dictionary* (1938), he is one of the first black celebs *not* compelled to come across as the stereotypical jabbering, eye-rolling Uncle Tom figure of Hollywood musicals. Primarily a band leader, in Hollywood Calloway sells himself on his vibrant personality, with such performances as the dapper high-rolling gambler (Yeller) in the Steve McQueen movie *The Cincinnati Kid*. As a singer, he's often pure vaudeville with a repertoire ranging from hop-head ditties like 'Reefer Man' and 'The Viper's Drag' through to his most famous of all recordings, 'Minnie The Moocher'. And who can forget 'Hotcha Razz-Ma-Tazz', 'Tarzan Of Harlem' and 'Chop-Chop Charlie Chan'?

But, if most of Cab's songs are forgettable, his suits hover eternally in the mind's eye. Dubbed 'zoot suits', these outrageous creations (using more material than a day bed), come heavily draped and wildly exaggerated.

Without doubt, Cab Calloway boasts Harlem's most expensive wardrobe. Legend has it – 40 suits with matching shoes. Cab's count is far greater. With one dozen costume changes commonplace in a single performance, Cab's investment is heavy, At a time when an off-the-peg zoot can sting the buyer for $33, Cab's cool-cat clobber ranges from a *cheap* $150 a garment to well over $250 for a *special*. When, in 1952, Cab Calloway becomes Sportin' Life in *Porgy And Bess*, it's pure typecasting.

Louis Jordan's career is one continuous Saturday night fish fry, establishing him as one of the most important (if historically neglected) figures in American black music. This excitable alto blowin' singer is to jump what Bird is to bop and Hendrix to rock; he defines the best aspects of the style in his own image. He exerts a profound influence on aspiring talents such as Ray Charles, Chuck Berry and B.B. King – the latter paying public tribute with reworks of Jordan's 'Inflation Blues' and 'Heed My Warning' on *Blues 'n' Jazz* (1983).

Whilst the combined might of the Tympany Five is engaged in reproducing a boogie-woogie pianist's pounding left-hand shuffle, Jordan self-mockingly shucks 'n' jives on the humorous side of sex and drugs and alcohol, whilst his penchant for overblowing his alto serves as a springboard for Earl Bostic who enjoys international recognition when pushing his raw rasping axe into tough tenor territory for King label hits 'Flamingo', 'Sleep' and 'Deep Purple'.

White imitators invariably fare much better than black originators, but Louis Jordan proves an exception. He makes Harlem jukebox records *and* sells them in their millions to middle-class whites rather than wealthy society slummers.

1944 – Louis Jordan even gets to make a chart-buster with Bing Crosby, 'Your Socks Don't Match'. Okay with the ofays, and with his own people even more of a hero. In a ten-year span that kicks off in 1942, Louis Jordan is seldom missing from the Harlem hit parade, and it isn't uncommon for him to enjoy three or four discs in the listings at any given moment. In 1946, he chalks up eleven straight hits. His unparalled popularity is further confirmed by the many movie shorts (*Caldonia*) and feature films (*Reet, Petite And Gone* and *Look Out Sister*) he makes to further promote his records. This even extends to a Tom and Jerry cartoon

(*Smitten Kitten*), using Jordan's 'Is You Is Or Is You Ain't My Baby?' as its soundtrack. Some of Jordan's three-minute 'soundies' become so popular, they received top billing over Hollywood's latest feature – often being run twice over at each performance.

Over the years, his best-known singles include million-plus sellers 'Choo-Choo Ch'Boogie' and 'Saturday Night Fish Fry' plus 'Let The Good Times Roll', 'Ain't Nobody Here But Us Chickens', 'Beware Brother Beware', 'What's The Use Of Getting Sober (When You're Gonna Get Drunk Again)', 'Five Guys Named Moe', 'Caldonia', 'GI Jive', 'Is You Is Or Is You Ain't My Baby', 'Buzz Me', two popular tracks with Ella Fitzgerald – 'Baby, It's Cold Outside' and 'Stone Cold Dead In The Market' – plus the massive 1947 hit, 'Open The Door, Richard'. Many of these are covered by everyone from Bill Haley and Dizzy Gillespie through to James Brown and Chuck Berry. Unquestionably, Van Morrison's single-only version of 'Caldonia' challenges Woody Herman's go-for-broke assault as the best-ever cover of a joyous Jordan jump.

Anyone searching for the roots of rock – its style, its self-deprecating humour, its unbridled drive – need look no further than Louis Jordan's Tympany Five.

Louis Jordan first learns his trade as a teenage hoofer and musician with the Rabbit Foot Minstrels – the outfit that gave Bessie Smith her start. He then tours with Ma Rainey, Queen Of The Blues, eventually becoming compere, vocalist and sideman with Chick Webb's Band, at the time that the little hunchback drummer's outfit is devastating Harlem's 'Home Of Happy Feet' – the Savoy Ballroom.

Situated on the second floor of a Lenox Avenue building, the Savoy occupies the entire front block between 140th and 141st streets. One night, Benny Goodman, the King Of Swing, arrives to challenge the resident Webb band. Four thousand Harlemites crowd into the ballroom. Another 5,000 are turned away at the door. And, on the two bandstands, a steamheat battle is fought. The Goodman orchestra, packed with jazz superstars, plays its heart out.

'Then,' reports *Metronome*, 'the men of Webb came back and blew the roof off the Savoy. The crowd screamed,

31

yelled and whistled with delirium.' After which, all bets are off.

'The Savoy was a place of tremendous enthusiasm and the home of fantastic dancing,' recollects pianist Mary Lou Williams. 'Webb was acknowledged king and any visiting band could depend upon catching hell from little Chick. He was a crazy drummer and shrewd to boot.'

Louis Thomas Jordan was just as shrewd. He learns all there is to know about sheer blues feel from Rainey; learns the art of cutting rival bands to shreds from the hunchback hero, Webb.

When Jordan quits Webb (1938), he's equipped to take on all-comers. He's perfected a vocal style that can woo whites, yet get the ghetto jukeboxes jumping. The siren call of his sax is just as distinctive – angry, yet streaked with a tinge of blue. Given the right material, he can hardly fail. The *right* material arrives in 1942.

By now, Jordan is leading his Tympany Five – usually a seven or eight strong outfit – playing white venues one week and black joints the next. He's amassed a number of hits in the race charts (black music discs usually emanate from a race or sepia series), but then he waxes 'GI Jive' and crosses over into the pop charts to go top five. It's not much of a song really. Just a hepper-than-thou ditty about army life, that runs:

'It's the GI Jive, man alive,

They wake you in the morning,

Blowin' reveille over your head.'

Happily, there are better things to come, including one of the most hilarious records ever to emerge from the whole R&B genre – 'Beware Brother Beware'. Jordan semi-raps crucial advice to would-be bachelors:

'When she calls you on the telephone

And asks, darling are you all alone?

Tell her, no – you've got three girls with you'

and

'If you go to a show

And she wants to sit in the back row,

Take her down front, take her *right* down front!'

Behind his vocal and the Five's shouts of encouragement, pianist Wild Bill Davis comps, the bassman walks, the drummer never stops swinging and the trumpeter and guitarist add neat fills, three horns locking to provide a tough opening come-on and final ride-out. On the face of things, an amusing record. It's brilliantly conceived, flawless, funny,

jumping, hot – the very essence of Tympany Five music.

Through such wild wax Jordan makes money. A lot of money. So much in fact, that he doesn't even complain when the kids outside the Apollo steal his hubcaps and sell them back to him. There's also the legend that whenever Jordan plays the Apollo, the place is so packed that some of the theatre's more enterprising employees (unbeknown to both artist and management) bolt in an extra row of seats, swiftly pocketing the unaccounted greenbacks.

Eventually, Jordan's luck *does* run out, the last Decca session being January 1954. A couple of months later, the company sign Bill Haley – a paunchy kiss-curled Philadelphian cowboy who has led such combos as The Saddlemen and The Four Aces Of Western Swing before switching to his particular brand of jump music. Decca place Haley in the care of producer Milt Gabler – the man who helped shape so many Jordan hits.

Gabler, sensing a potentially massive WASP market for a blanched counterpart, moulds Haley as the Great White Hope. He remembers: 'I'd sing Jordan riffs to the group (The Comets) that would be picked up by the electric guitars and tenor sax of Rudy Pompelli. They got a sound that had the drive of the Tympany Five and the colour of country and western.'

Despite phenomenal initial response, Haley's Comet burns itself out in double-quick time, after which he goes into the nostalgia business, eventually dying a crazed man. Louis Jordan, the originator, neglected as the rockers take over the teen world, claims it's just another case of mighty whitey taking over.

'Rock 'n' roll was not a marriage of R&B and country and western', Jordan explains to writer Arnold Shaw. 'Rock 'n' roll was just a white imitation, a white adaptation of Negro R&B.' It will take until the beginning of the eighties for the facts to be fully corrected in Louis Jordan's favour.

And Bill Haley isn't the only straw-grabber to recycle Jordan's choice licks. Chuck Berry, Ray Charles and, to a lesser extent, Nat 'King' Cole testify to the man's influence.

In later years, Nat 'King' Cole may well enjoy the role of crooner, but in 1940 (when signed to Decca), he heads a jumpy little trio cutting sides like 'Hit That Jive, Jack'. As Cole's career develops, he's heard leading a rhythm section (featuring innovative electric guitarist Les Paul) that gives ground support to the notorious Illinois Jacquet – Jack McVea 'Jazz At The Philharmonic' tenor sax battles –

Louis Jordan

Left to right: *Lionel Hampton, Jack McVea, Ella 'n' Illinois, Hamp and Chamblee*

horn-to-horn confrontations, taking on all the furore of a main event title fight that, on occasion, climax in genuine blood-letting.

'There were a lotta good tenor players around,' admits one of their number – 'Bullmoose' Jackson. 'Cutting contests were fun, but if you had any sense you'd avoid going up against Illinois – *that* man was the Joe Louis of the tenor . . . *un-beatable*!'

A watertight case for the genesis of rock 'n' roll taking place in LA on 2 July 1944 can be backed by evidence contained on a JATP recording of 'Blues', during which Jacquet and McVea square off against one another in one almighty showdown of skill, excess and endurance.

'Cacophony,' reports the *Melody Maker* man on the spot.

'More!' yells the audience, who indulge in the ritual of chanting 'Oi, Oi, Oi' whenever the saxmen seize one note and proceed to wring it out.

Hard on the heels of Hampton, Jordan and Jacquet come innumerable jubilant jivers, jumpers and jitterbugs. Out on the coast, Exclusive come up with Joe Liggins and his Honey drippers and their appropriately named 'The Honey-dripper' which, in 1945, is the first jump instrumental to

claim one million sold. Another LA independent, Juke Box (later renamed Specialty), hit the following year with Roy Milton and his Solid Senders' 'RM Blues' – stylistically innovative and, to date, the biggest record in urban black music. Meanwhile, the New Jersey-located Savoy set-up quickly follow through with hard-hitting baritone saxist Paul Williams' 'The Hucklebuck' – replete with lyrics. The cover version from baggy-suited, bow-tied Frank Sinatra ensures this finger-snapper extra airplay. Thrill again to Sinatra's aside, 'Not now Moose, I'll tell ya when', followed by the encouraging cry, 'Right now, Dad' as 'Bullmoose' Jackson burps a fashionable tenor solo.

Jump never really strays too far away from the influence of such eight-to-the-bar boogie-woogie Steinway strokers as Meade Lux Lewis, Albert Ammons and Pete Johnson. Keyboard kings are next in line behind jump's tenor titans. Amos Milburn – leader of the Chickenshackers – runs a tight second to Joe Liggins as a style-setting chartbuster, after

notching up gold with 'Chicken Shack Boogie' (Aladdin). His finger-buster style – like New Orleans' Professor Longhair – shapes Fats Domino's career, along with those of Floyd Dixon and Little Willie Littlefield, the man whose piano triplets help blueprint the more commercial design of mid-fifties R&B.

Contrary to Wilbert Harrison's disclosure, there's much more than just 'crazy little women' to be savoured in Kansas City – America's most open Sin City, where gangster Tom Pendergast runs over 500 pleasure palaces where a man can go mad for just five dollars. The other attractions in town are the Shouters – liquor-lovin' men like Jimmy Rushing, Walter Brown, and Jimmy Witherspoon who roar out the blues. Boss of 'em all, and billed that way, is 'Big' Joe Turner.

A 250-pound bartender by vocation, Turner stands behind the bar of the Sunset Club simultaneously serving up groove-juice and belting out the blues to Pete Johnson's piano accompaniment. Though he inspires almost as many vocalists as Louis Jordan, Turner's early years pass largely unappreciated outside of KC.

Turner is to cash in during the early days of rock 'n' roll. An Atlantic label artist, he cuts the smash 1954 hit 'Shake,

Rattle And Roll', only to be promptly covered by Bill Haley, who moves the song's original setting from the boudoir to the kitchen!

Wynonie Harris idolized 'Big' Joe Turner, to the point of moving from Omaha to the 'Heavenly City' so as to learn his craft first hand from Turner and other local stars. The doyen of the *double-entendre*, it's but a short time before 'Mr Blues' (as Harris now calls himself) has his own chart-topper, 'All She Wants To Do is Rock (Rock 'n' Roll All Night Long)'.

Wynonie Harris truly walks it like he talks it, with such lascivious sides as 'Don't Roll Those Bloodshot Eyes At Me', 'Adam Come And Get Your Rib', 'Lovin' Machine' (a cover of protégé Roy Brown's 'Good Rockin' Tonight) plus 'I Love My Baby's Pudding', which isn't about either rice or sago!

Presley, for one, copped his carnal contortions watching Wynonie's many Memphis appearances, but fails to check out how to make the Grand Exit. When, in 1969, Wynonie realizes he can't lick the Big C, he draws out all his money from the bank, jets in all his friends to his Oakland home, parties non-stop for well over a week then, when the guests split, cleans up the debris, goes upstairs and dies peacefully in his sleep.

Now *that's* style.

A SHOT OF
RHYTHM 'N' BLUES

Rhythm 'n' blues boomed out of southern California in the brief respite between the termination of World War Two and the outbreak of the Korean conflict.

The rapid expansion of US defence-project industries prompted two million workers rapidly to relocate along the West Coast. A large proportion were black, Texan (or thereabouts), unexpectedly prosperous and allowed easy access to what (prior to Pearl Harbor) were white-only clubs, saloons and hangouts. These newly-affluent migrants wanted music that reflected their sudden upward mobility. Definitely *not* on their checklist were wheezing harp country blues produced by those major labels still smarting both from lengthy union bans on recording and from a vinyl shortage.

The demand for new music was there – supplying it, a different matter. Cutting a half-decent R&B session wasn't without obstacles. For example, it wasn't unknown for record dates to be convened at a friendly bordello simply because, other than the neighbourhood storefront church, the local sporting house possessed the only usable upright. That problem solved, getting records pressed was almost an impossibility.

Though the converted were prepared to pay over a dollar a disc, against the 50 or 70 cents asked by the majors, few records were getting through to the shops for, despite acquiring 75 per cent of all new R&B releases, jukebox operators still demanded even more product to feed their money-making machines. Furthermore, Pullman car porters were fattening their wallets 'exporting' each week's hot sounds to Chicago and beyond for up to ten dollars a biscuit.

No matter how persuasive they were, even the most palm-greasing independent record outfits had to contend with the fact that LA's major-owned plants – obsessed with maintaining their status – were reluctant to custom-press more than 200 discs each week for the queues of cash-only entrepreneurs. And the actual process of pressing records was an even more guarded secret than plans for the latest Sabre jets.

It was to take one thousand greenbacks – the cost of covertly assembling LA's first independent pressing plant – to smash the majors' monopoly and flood the dollar-drenched West Coast with this new nickel-spinning jump. The million-plus sales for Private Cecil Gant's 'I Wonder' (Gilt Edge), in 1945, was the impetus required. The big four majors realized that their supremacy had been challenged and that it was too late to take effective action.

All the black music stars such as Johnny Moore's Three

Good Rockin' Tonite Man – Roy Brown

Blazers (featuring Charles Brown), Amos Milburn, T-Bone Walker, Lowell Fulsom, Ivory Joe Hunter, Johnny Otis, Pee Wee Crayton, Jesse Belvin, B.B. King, Joe Liggins and Roy Milton and his Solid Senders were then able to emerge through such hole-in-the-wall set-ups such as Aladdin, Specialty, Modern, Black & White, Exclusive and Excelsior.

This was the era when the most influential popular black music entertainers were record stars Louis Jordan and Nat 'King' Cole – personifying, as they did, a new sophistication prevalent amongst blacks only too eager to disassociate themselves from what they branded 'field nigger' music. Louis Jordan offered a potently humorous concoction of jump, jive and bebop, while Nat 'King' Cole's trio were prime purveyors of club blues – a smooth blend of subtle blues and boom-time Hollywood glamour customized for the after-hours clubs that quietly ignored California's 2.00 am last call for alcohol.

Whereas, in recent times, popular music is often created in a vacuum and for no other tangible purpose than endorsing trinkets, forties R&B was an authentic experience – its immediacy infectious; its edge the sharpest. A song, having been tried and tested nightly by the likes of Jordan, Milburn or Fulsom, might have already achieved hit status before its transference to hot wax.

Hollywood's burgeoning R&B clubland didn't offer rich pickings for the big bands, many of whose swing had all but swung. As with bebop, limited seating capacity and basic economics created a new breed of compact entertainment. Louis Jordan's Tympany Five had already shown the door to any sixteen men swingin', and club-owners reasoned that trimmed-to-the-bone versions of the Lionel Hampton and Lucky Millinder orchestras should receive immediate consideration.

Roy Milton's Solid Senders and the Johnny Otis Band demonstrated that they could kick up almost as much dust as threefold their number (though in time they too would be replaced by even smaller tenor/organ combos). Similarly, the now-in-demand 'drumless' after-hours trios of Nat 'King' Cole, Johnny Moore and Ivory Joe Hunter offered a smooth alternative to those all-night cutting contests where bar-walking tenormen secretly slipped sulphates into each other's drinks, then stepped aside as their adversaries short-circuited in a brain-blasting barrage of honks, squeals and screams.

The curse of the after-hours clubowner wasn't how many times the bartender resold the same drink, but that, in such glamorous surroundings, sophisticats wanted only their cocktails and not their conversations shaken. As a result, the music was blues-soft and ballad-bound, and, should the joint jump, it was rhythmic rather than percussive. This unique brand of club-blues was exquisitely styled by the Nat 'King' Cole Trio. Though voted, amongst other things, Downbeat magazine's Top Small Combo between 1944-7, Cole wasn't without stiff competition.

Texas-born Charles Brown started out as pianist with Johnny Moore's Three Blazers (themselves modelled on the 'King' Cole Trio), but his penchant for introspective self-pitying deep-blue ballads such as 'Drifting Blues' and 'Merry Christmas Baby' made him one of the undisputed idols of the era. Whereas Cole crossed-over into popdom, Brown's cool elegance greatly influenced such aspiring contenders as Amos Milburn and Ray Charles.

Johnny Moore's Three Blazers featuring Charles Brown (extreme right)

CROONERS, SWOONERS
AND
FLAT-TOP FLIPPERS

Sinatra was the first of the ofay sharpies. While Bing Crosby aimed unerringly at the family, Francis Albert, the kid from Hoboken, sang on behalf of Young America.

Crosby, in reality, wasn't *that* unhip. He'd done his rebel run bit during his younger days. Even blew his first major singing role in a movie because he'd got himself stuck in an LA jail. Musically too, he'd hardly been an equilateral rectangle. He'd recorded an exceptional version of 'St Louis Blues' in the august company of Duke Ellington. Many of his other records featured jazzmen of quality and, as R&B caught hold, he moved on to cut sides with the likes of Louis Jordan and Lionel Hampton's big band. Nevertheless, to the kids of the mid-forties, El Bingo still seemed the guy most likely to end up singing hits to nuns.

Not that Sinatra was really the answer to a bobbysoxer's dream. For a start, at the time of his first solo hit he was twenty-eight and lying about his age. But the then thin man's publicity machine, adroitly supervised by agent George Evans, created the myth of Sinatra as the Sultan of Swoon, thus helping to create hysteria among the kids who attended Sinatra's concerts. The knock-on effect was, predictably, that most of middle-aged America reared in anger. 'He's the main reason for the rise in juvenile delinquency,' some claimed. Such anger, in turn, guaranteed Sinatra's total acceptance by the kids, who saw the ex-Dorsey band singer as their personal provider of teen dreams, the guy who equated gliss with kiss.

It wasn't only that he phrased and sang like nobody else on the block. Frank was a fashion-leader, too. When he began wearing his floppy bow-ties, some made by Sulka's, some by his wife, sales of neckware increased by 400 per cent. And when he once rolled up the sleeves of his jacket during a public appearance, thousands of teenies followed suit. There was a Sinatra language, too, one in which the word 'hey' was used as a kind of punctuation. 'A hubba, hubba, Frankie, hey!' habitually cheered his fans, thus pre-empting the Ramones' 'Gabba, gabba, gabba, hey!' by light years.

Sinatra was not just another bony baritone. To the kids who queued for hours to see him appear onstage at the New

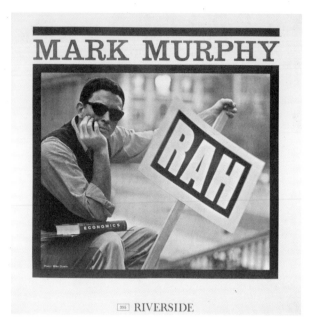

York Paramount, he represented a whole new reason to believe.

Thing was, though, that Sinatra really *could* sing. Not in a play-to-the-gallery, blast-the-high-notes way – even if his range has always been impressive enough. It was the way he phrased a song, something that he'd learnt in his years with the big bands, that stunned those who heard beyond the bobby soxers' screams. Sinatra has since said that he tried to 'play' his voice, like jazz musicians play their instruments. And while he's sometimes come unstuck when attempting to grandstand in front of a roaring big band like Count Basie's, Sinatra, in the main, has proved the master of the seamless phrase, Mr Swing Easy Inc.

Next to Sinatra, Dick Haymes was the man to follow. Come to think of it, he was always *next* to Frank. When Frank upped and left the Harry James band, in 1940, it was the Argentine-born Haymes who was chosen to replace him. And when Hoboken's finest finally split from Tommy Dorsey a couple of years later, Haymes was once again hauled off the sub's bench. Even then, it didn't end. In 1955 he signed with Capitol Records, the label that had signed Sinatra just two years earlier.

Haymes never sounded in the least like Sinatra, though. His was a deeper, richer voice, yet intimate. He'd never bawl if a whisper would suffice; his was the arm-round-the-shoulder approach. Warm. Comforting. Like Sinatra, he could lose much of his subtlety when shoved out in front of a powerhouse brass section. But, given the unpretentious

arrangements provided by arrangers Johnny Mandel and Ian Bernard on such albums as *Moondreams* and *Rain or Shine*, Haymes was the perfect balladeer, the ultimate romantic turn-on.

And turn on women Haymes undoubtedly could. He married singers Edith Harper and Fran Jeffries (later, a Playboy centrefold at the age of 40); film actresses Joanne Dru and Rita 'the Body' Hayworth; Errol Flynn's ex-wife Nora; and, finally, model Wendy Patricia Smith. Unfortunately, for many years Haymes himself was turned-on by booze and turned-off by tax bills, most of which he neglected to pay.

Then, he never chose the easy way. Once he blacked Rita Hayworth's eye and was consequently sued flat in the divorce court. For years he fought an on-and-off battle with the US Immigration Department, who were constantly attempting to have him deported. On an Australian trip, he was sacked from an engagement because of 'unprofessional conduct', and in 1971 shook out his piggy-bank, only to be declared bankrupt. Then in March 1981 came the one that Haymes couldn't win. Cancer claimed another victim. But just before his death, the one-time stuntman – he was the guy that dived 75 feet from the mast in the Charles Laughton classic *Mutiny On The Bounty* – cut one last album, *As Time Goes By*. It proved to be among his best. So Haymes died as he had lived. In considerable style.

If Sinatra and Haymes can be considered as the Coleman Hawkins and Ben Webster of vocalists, then Mel

Torme is an ever-swinging Charlie Parker. A twenty-nine-year-old baby-face, he led his vocal group, the Mel-Tones, on Artie Shaw's 1946 waxing of 'What Is This Thing Called Love' and blew all other existing vocal combos out of sight. Possessor of a smokey vocal style which has seen him dubbed 'The Velvet Fog', Torme not only sings but arranges, produces, writes, acts, and plays both piano and drums. Despite such a truckful of talent his on-record hit tally is pitifully small, his biggest boost in this area being an unlikely British top ten hit with a version of Rodgers and Hart's 'Mountain Greenery'. Not surprisingly, Torme has toted something of a chip on his shoulder for many years, gaining a reputation for being surly because of lack of recognition. 'I still try and avoid reading reviews', he claimed recently, owning up that he bruises easily.

Now, perhaps, the younger generation has at last cottoned on to Torme's vocal genius. In 1983, The Creatures, an outfit formed by Siouxsie Sioux and Budgie of The Banshees, successfully revived 'Comin' Home, Baby', a vocal version of a Herbie Mann number which Mel turned into a hit during 1963, while Was (Not Was), an eclectic New York funk band, also had thoughts of Torme that same year, hauling him into the studio to perform 'Zaz Turned Blue', a song on their much-hailed *Born To Laugh At Tornadoes* album. 'We had the song, but couldn't imagine how to bring it off,' David Was later told reporter David Keeps, his 'brother' Don Was adding: 'Having Mel record it was beyond our wildest dreams. He sang it this one time and it was one of the

heaviest moments of my musical life because he sang the piss out of the song!'

As always.

One odd thing about Torme. Nobody, but nobody, tried to imitate him.

Sinatra, on the other hand, inspired countless clones, followers, and others who pilfered the odd phrase or two. Johnny Desmond, a fine singer who worked for Glenn Miller's AEF Band, became known as the GI Sinatra, while Vic Damone, another popular vocalist whose efforts have sometimes been spoilt by operatics, was tagged 'the second Sinatra', and admitted: 'Sure I copied Sinatra, who didn't? I used to save my money for those 25 cent record-your-voice machines and practised singing just like Frank.'

Over the years, there have been scores of singers who have reflected the Sinatra vocal way of things – singers like Tony Travis, Johnny Janis, Frankie Lester, Julius La Rosa, Frankie Randall and Steve Lawrence (the last-named, when not making wimpy records with his wife, Eydie Gorme, proving technically more proficient than most). Guitar-playing Frank D'Rone was another of the more inventive singers to handle a Sinatra lick. Then, time and time again, the singing musicians of the forties and fifties frequently showed that they were more capable of turning mere songs

into musical experiences than such accredited crooners as ex-barber Perry Como or even Andy Williams (a singer who, at one point, provided the on-screen singing voice of Lauren Bacall!).

Matt Dennis was one such supper-club hipster. A piano-playing product of the same Tommy Dorsey aggregation that produced Frank Sinatra and Buddy Rich, he sang in a warm relaxed style and wrote songs like 'Angel Eyes', 'Violets For Your Furs' and 'Everything Happens To Me', all of which were turned into classics by Sinatra, who once proclaimed himself 'President of the Hoboken Local of the Matt Dennis Fan Club'. Bobby Troup, whose career receives due mention elsewhere was another who played piano as if he meant it and sang songs so well that you wondered why he bothered to pound a keyboard in the first place.

And there were others. Like piano-playing Cy Coleman, another supper-club regular who provided Sinatra with great songs, before going on to write shows such as *Barnum* and *Sweet Charity*. Like blind accordionist Joe Mooney, ex-Goodman pianist Buddy Greco, guitar-player Jackie Paris and keyboardist Bobby Scott. Like gum-chewing drummers Buddy Rich and Ray McKinley, trumpet star Chet Baker and a score or more who not only played instruments but also proffered vocals that musically dug you in the ribs.

Right back at the beginning though, there was Hoagy. Hoagland Howard Carmichael, to give him his full name. A sometime cornet-player from Bloomington, Indiana, he switched to full-time piano and composed scores of classic songs ('Stardust', 'Georgia On My Mind', 'Lazy River'...), but became more widely accepted as a singer during the forties, when his movie roles, mainly portraying the world's most lethargic saloon pianists, brought him to the notice of a whole new audience. His was an oddball voice, all hominy grits and slow to deliver. But even on the most turgid of novelty tunes his jazz feel always peeked through, a trait he shared with his one-time co-writer Johnny Mercer, a singer-composer who made so much money from songs like 'That Old Black Magic' and 'Blues In The Night' that he was able to form Capitol Records.

Perhaps the main link between then and now is Mose Allison, a singer-pianist who, though born in 1927, didn't make his first record until well into the rock era. Mainly influenced by such pianists as Erroll Garner and Nat Cole – he even played one gig as 'Nat Garner' – he in turn has influenced Georgie Fame, Randy Newman, Ben Sidran and Michael Franks, all modern-day keyboardists who have a

yen to test their tonsils on blues and associated hues. Once tackled about his debt to Carmichael, Allison said: 'We both have a similar vocal sound and, of course, he was one of the few people who was a singing piano-player. We have, too, the same kind of accent and we both came from the same part of the States. Then, I've also had an audience who'd say: "Hey, you've been listening to Randy Newman." The similarity as I see it is the satirical approach we both use and the laconic kind of songs we perform. If anybody sees a similarity between Randy and myself, then that's fine with me.'

So who's left among the Great Whites?

Tony Bennett? Well, maybe. Certainly, like Crosby, he's more aware than many people have ever given him credit for. He's recorded with Basie, Art Blakey, Ralph Sharon, Bill Evans, Bobby Hackett and, more often than not, picked songs that reek of class. Yet, somehow, he doesn't really fit. Unlike Fred Astaire. When great singers are mentioned, nobody talks about Astaire except the singers themselves. Tony Bennett says: 'I really dig Fred Astaire as a singer, he's just wonderful', while Torme has cited the former Frederick Austerlitz as his all-time favourite vocalist, and jazz impresario Norman Granz was so taken by Astaire's ability to make a lyric dance that, in 1953, he talked the Hollywood hoofer into a set of records on which Astaire was backed by members of Jazz At The Philharmonic. In reality, Astaire who, incidentally, recorded some tracks for the world's first 33⅓ rpm long-players (made by RCA in 1931) – hasn't *that* much of a singing voice. His tone's thin and his range limited. But he projects a lyric better than just about anyone else around and, when provided with swinging backing, vocally skips across the beat like a hot horn player.

'White singers, singing like blacks – people like Bing Crosby and Johnny Mercer, Hoagy Carmichael, even Fred Astaire – were the first real hipsters', avers David Frishberg, a singer-songwriter considered pretty hip himself in some circles. 'They were the first to absorb the essence of what the black singers were doing. In their work from the early thirties, you could hear the black influence on rhythm come creeping into the culture. Then you hear it come out when they are not trying to ape black singers or imitate the accent, but are absorbing it into a style, rather than a black-face, vaudeville thing. These singers use black, rhythmic things to express themselves musically, not in order to sound like a black person.'

Fred Astaire, bless his spats, is alreeet!

THE SEPIA SINATRAS

The ebony crooners. Tall, black and handsome. The outfront guys with velvet-clad tonsils and sex appeal apparently ebbing from their gullets. You didn't have to see them at a dance hall or club to know how they looked. To hear them on disc or over the radio was enough. They were the dream-weavers, the spell-casters, the ones who made it abundantly clear exactly what lay at the end of every female's rainbow.

Who knows who was first? Certainly they pre-dated Francis Albert, under whose name they were later to be categorized. Pha Terrell, for one, proved a punter-puller way back in 1936. Boy Wonder with Andy Kirk's Clouds Of Joy, he emoted so sensationally on a song called 'Until The Real Thing Comes Along' that the resulting record became the black music single of the year.

Dempsey J. Travis, in his book *An Autobiography Of Jazz*, recalls:

When the song hit the jukeboxes across the country, the Kirk Band became an overnight sensation. On the Sunday night that Kirk appeared at the Chicago Savoy, you could hardly get near the place. People must have been turned away by the thousand. The dance was to start at seven. It was hell inside and people were jammed in that ballroom like boat people. And when Pha Terrell opened his mouth to sing 'I've worked for you, I've slaved for you . . .' everyone went wild. Terrell would repeat that opening stanza before going into the bridge of the song in a high falsetto— and the girls went wild, and so did the men. I've never experienced anything like that in my life.

Herb Jeffries, who joined Duke Ellington's band in early 1940, and Billy Eckstine, who became vocalist with Earl Hines around the same time, both provided their new employers with massive hits within months of getting their first pay cheques. Both were hunky, handsome, light-skinned baritones with voices that eased gently between blues and bedroom. Jeffries made his bid with 'Flamingo' and instantly became the most popular male singer Ellington ever possessed, while Eckstine first tumbled into the way-ward thoughts of America's black womanhood via 'Jelly, Jelly', a blues he and Hines had slotted together in just twelve minutes. Nearly forty years later, The Allman Brothers recorded the song and Hines and Eckstine suddenly found themselves some 40,000 dollars better off through a sudden unexpected influx of royalties.

If Jeffries faltered after quitting the big band scene, Eckstine, whose real name was Eckstein before somebody felt that a black man with a Jewish name might be doubly hard to take, continued moving on and up. A fair trombone and trumpet player, he initially formed his own band. But it wasn't just a band. The line-up was more a listing of exactly

APPEARING NIGHTLY
Classic Supper Club
PRESENTS
Mr. Billy Eckstine

Top: *Charles Brown*   Middle: *Ray Charles*
Bottom: *Al Hibbler*   Right: *Billy Eckstine*

who was going to make it in the world of jazz during the years ahead. Miles Davis, Dizzy Gillespie, Fats Navarro, Art Blakey, Gene Ammons, Sonny Stitt, Dexter Gordon, Kenny Dorham, Charlie and Leo Parker, Wardell Gray, Sarah Vaughan – all helped Eckstine make great music and lose money in the mid-forties. Then one day he decided that enough was enough.

'The band was into bebop and you can't sing so well with that', he opined. 'I decided to go single and go hear Dizzy for kicks.' So he went solo, signed for the new MGM label and deposited his wide vibrato over ballads like 'I Apologise' and 'Everything I Have Is Yours'. He had hit after hit and moved into Esther Williams bathing epics, parading his Mr B roll-collar shirts and his array of drapes for the appraisal of big screen buffs. And, for a while, it seemed that every cat worth his sartorial salt latched on to Mr B's lead. Vocally, he made it too. In the polls that mattered, he even eclipsed Sinatra himself for several years in a row. But, even then, nobody got around to calling Frank a Caucasian Eckstine.

After Herb Jeffries left Ellington's band, Duke signed a blind singer from Little Rock, called Al Hibbler. Hardly a smoothie like Jeffries, Hibbler possessed the most oddball vocal style on the big band circuit. He phrased curiously, filled songs with unlikely vocal swoops and employed a line of pronunciation that sounded almost Cockney-influenced at times. The songs he sang with Duke were often almost as unlikely – squelchy, old folks' faves like 'Trees' and 'Danny Boy'. Yet he fascinated. Everytime he sang, it was aurally like watching a faltering tightrope walker. Often he seemed as if he was heading for musical disaster. Then, just as you expected him to fall flat on his fanny, he'd toss in something that grabbed you by the ears and pinned you to the wall. As successful as he was individual, eventually he too went solo and in 1955 had a million-seller with a classic version of 'Unchained Melody'.

While some played it rugged and mildly macho, others adopted a softer, after-hours approach, following in the path of Nat Cole. One such performer was a singing piano-player from Nashville who answered to the name of Cecil Gant. A serviceman, in late 1944 he recorded some sides for Gilt Edge as Pvt. Cecil Gant, the label promoting him as 'The GI Sing-Sation'. Then one of his cuts, a simple, blues-tinged ballad that answered to the name of 'I Wonder', broke BIG. Soon it was one of the fastest selling black singles in America – all the more remarkable because it was on an indie label at a time when the 'die' part of the nomenclature seemed more relevant than the 'in'. To promote it further, Gant, dressed in army issue gear and coming on like a human Victory Bond, began touring, establishing house records in venues right across the country. Eventually 'I Wonder' claimed million-selling status. But Gant faded almost as quickly as he'd arrived. Even an exchange of suits didn't help. But, for a while at least, he'd made khaki ultra-cool.

Also influenced by Cole plus Pha Terrell was Charles Brown, a sometime schoolboy cocktail pianist who became vocalist with Johnny Moore's Three Blazers. An easytime-blues specialist who smoothed out the edges of twelve-bars and made them slot alongside Martinis and nightclub memories, Brown, together with The Blazers, had a 1946 million-seller with 'Drifting Blues'. Unlike Gant, however, Brown wasn't destined for the ranks of the one-hit wonders. He went solo and continued his winning ways on wax for many years, contributing an array of romantic, blues-ballad hits. And just when everybody was writing him off in 1961, he came up with a massive cross-over hit, 'Please Come Home For Christmas', that proved so enduring that The Eagles decided to revive it, successfully, during the sock-to-the-bedpost season in 1978.

The list of those who could qualify as Sepia Sinatras seems endless. Such a tally might contain the names of Ivory Joe Hunter, perhaps the first black singer really to merge blues with country; Johnny Hartman, a fine balladeer whose list of recordings includes dates in the company of John Coltrane; Joe Williams, another sophisticated bluesman, whose presence added greatly to the Basie band's pulling power during the mid-fifties; and others like Roy Hamilton, Adam Wade, Brook Benton, Freddie Cole, and even Ray Charles and Oscar Peterson, both of whom have made albums that suggest Nat Cole once left his tonsils over at their house. Of the host of would-be's, many made it, many didn't. Some were mainstream men for a while, others didn't even get an invitation to attend the opening ceremony at vinyl valhalla.

Unluckiest of the brood? Possibly Johnny Ace, whose warm and tear-pervaded style edged him nearer than most to being the ultimate cross-over singer, the one who would merge black and white into a glorious shade of grey and take the result into both the Apollo and the Waldorf-Astoria without selling out to either side. He seemed capable of so much. When Duke put out his record of 'Pledging My Love'

in 1955, it leapt out of the black music charts and right into the pop top twenty. But Ace had already gone. Playing a game of Russian Roulette on Christmas Eve 1954, he came out a loser, leaving just a host of might-have-beens and the basis for a Paul Simon song.

Others argue that Jesse Belvin might have been even bigger. Nancy Wilson once proclaimed: 'If I had to choose just one album it would be one of Jesse Belvin's', and the one-time LA R&B genius is claimed as an influence by many. Signed to RCA in late 1958, he was placed in the hands of arrangers like Shorty Rogers and Marty Paich and groomed to provide the label's answer to the all-conquering Cole. But his chauffeur was one Charles Ford, a man sacked by Ray Charles because of his erratic driving. In February 1960, while Belvin was on his way to a Dallas date, he was killed when his Ford-driven car suddenly swerved into the wrong lane and crashed head-on into a vehicle travelling the opposite way. Maybe such early deaths have helped keep the Ace and Belvin reputations intact. Because they went when they were ahead on all counts, they'll undoubtedly remain heroes. Maybe if they'd have lived, they might have faded into anonymity or, more probably, as they struggled to maintain an audience, they might have been adjudged pure MOR, fellow-travellers of Johnny Mathis, himself once a name bandied around in circles given to comparing the note-filled tumbles of Fats Navarro with the more sparing, economic forays of an up-and-coming Miles.

Some are hip in their own time. Some stay hip forever. The only rule is that there are no rules.

COOL COLE

Right: *The Nat King Cole Trio*
Left: *Nat and Babs*

The tall black man, onstage, swung into the final chorus of 'Little Girl'. 'Little girl, you're the one girl for me', he sang, phrasing the age-old Hyde and Henry song like a jazzman.

Suddenly, menacing figures loomed out of the audience. Armed with knuckle-dusters, blackjacks and bottles, they headed for the stage. As a woman screamed, the Klansman grabbed at the singer over the footlights. The microphone toppled, smashing the victim full in the face, sending him staggering back against the piano. The supporting band, trying to quell the panic, began playing the national anthem but, being a visiting British aggregation, they played theirs. 'To hell with the Queen, drop the curtain', yelled somebody backstage. All was chaos.

And so ended Nat 'King' Cole's return to his home state.

These days, Nathanial Adams Coles is usually remembered as something of a wimp, a family favourite given to mush-mouthing saccharine ballads like 'Faith Can Move Mountains' or ukelele-accompanied candyfloss like 'Lazy, Hazy Days of Summer'. And maybe, to some extent, that's what he became.

But it wasn't always that way.

Initially, he was not only a balladeer of superior quality but also someone wise to a line of jive, an R&B regent whose piano playing alone enabled him to win polls and influence the penny-pushers at the jumpiest jukeboxes in town.

Recalling the early Nat Cole Trio in his book *The Great American Popular Singers*, critic Henry Pleasants claimed: 'In those days when the star had been, initially at least, the pianist rather than the vocalist, I thought to myself: "This guy can play more piano standing up than most pianists can play sitting down and he can do more singing sitting down than most singers do standing up!"'

The son of a preacher, Cole, from Montgomery, Alabama, but raised mainly on Chicago's South Side, learnt his trade playing a piano and organ in his father's church. The product of a family of musicians – his brothers Eddie, Isaac and Freddie all paid their jazz dues – Nat Cole hardly had any other way to go. He led a Chicago outfit known as The Royal Dukes for a while, became a sideman with his brother Eddie's band and, in 1937, formed the first version of The King Cole Trio, a combo that proved to be a ground-breaker with its piano, electric guitar and bass line-up.

Among the first to realize the group's potential was Lionel Hampton. He hauled the threesome into the studio to back his stomping vibes and two-fingered piano antics on such 1940 R&B specials as 'Jivin' With Jarvis' and 'Jack The Bellboy'. That same year, the Trio began cutting their own Decca sides, mainly tossing up catchy, light-weight, R&B riffs on which Cole's own imaginative piano choruses vied for attention with the equally innovative playing of guitarist Oscar Moore. But it was the vocals that caught the ear of the non-jazzers. It's said that one cut, a softly-rendered slice of blues-hued romance known as 'This Will Make You Laugh', would have been Cole's first hit but for the fact that Decca, hit by wartime shortages, were unable to provide enough materials to press up orders. From then on, it was the long wait until 1944 before the King Cole Trio eventually clambered up the pop charts, the eventual tote for the top coming with 'Straighten Up and Fly Right'. It was the kind of jivey do-dab that the group had been playing for years.

But if the Cole Trio had been one of a kind at the start, its success sparked a whole regime of piano-guitar-and-bass totin' rivals such as Johnny Moore's Three Blazers, the Page Cavanaugh Trio and the Soft Winds, vocalists that included Charles Brown and, later, Ray Charles and Oscar Peterson matching the Cole vocal style, nuance for nuance. But international success proved the beginning of the end for Cole, R&B's gentle persuader.

Increasingly, he worked with studio orchestras, string sections, vocal choruses, and, by 1951, had completely dispensed with the trio. He still sang better than most – and he never completely forgot his jazz roots. Just when you'd written him off, he'd jump back with a blues or an album that allowed him to jam with Juan Tizol, Willie Smith, Stuff Smith and 'Sweets' Edison. But, give or take a track or two, Cole was vying for *Metronome* and *Downbeat* honours no more. He made it into movies, became the first black to front his own TV show, made a lot of money and helped other worthy causes do the same, raising over $50,000 for civil rights groups and also helping to net nearly $130,000 in an attempt to revoke California's anti-discrimination housing laws, thus setting himself up as a target for Klansmen while on Southern touring duties.

But it wasn't the Klan but the Big C that eventually silenced one of R&B's most influential voices. A tall rangy man, one day he found that his belt was loose. He had an extra hole punched and tightened it. A little later he was forced to punch an extra hole, then another. And one night in February 1965 it simply didn't matter anymore.

TONSILS
AND
TOGETHERNESS

AN EVERYDAY STORY OF HIPSTERS IN HARMONY

The Mel-Tones were the first to break the smooth harmony hold of the Pied Pipers, the Modernaires and the other groups who'd lent vocal pzazz to the big bands during the war years. Formed by the teenage Mel Torme, the Mel-Tones yelped 'Bop baio, bop baio' at the intro to Artie Shaw's Musicraft waxing of 'What Is This Thing Called Love' in 1946 and thus announced the coming of a new era in vocal sounds.

It was also the end of an age. The parent bands that spawned the groups couldn't afford to keep them on the payroll. Before long, most of the harmony heroes were making it on their own. The King Sisters quit Alvino Rey, the Clark Sisters split from Tommy Dorsey and even the lesser known Blue Moods moved out from the protection of the Herman Herd to become the Skylarks. They were all part of a musical élite. Give them a note and they'd immediately wrap it in so many musical dressings that you'd imagine that Dior was into clef-work.

Then, from out of the crowd came two groups that made even the most talented of their competitors seem like amateur night at the local hop. The first was the Four Freshmen who, during the fifties, not only introduced a harmony style that acted as a vocal counterpart to Kenton's Progressive Jazz movement, but also proved to be able musicians, capable of handling trombone, french horn, trumpet, mellophone, guitar, bass and drum parts. It was hardly unexpected when they zapped all the polls.

But if the Freshmen were sensational, the Ivy League clad Hi-Los were totally unbelievable. After Gene Puerling, their ace chartsman, arranged a song, it was never quite the same again. They'd take a show tune like 'Surrey With The Fringe On Top' and turn it inside out. They'd handle it like an oddball lullaby, tossing in strange harmonies, totally irrational phrases that made you gasp at their audaciousness. Then they'd stomp off at breakneck pace, punctuating the flow of things by means of simulated trumpet shakes, with Clark Burroughs' skyscraper falsetto apparently travelling where no man had ever gone before. They were humorous, and could afford to be. They were the vocal equivalent of Pele, arrogant, entertaining, able to toy with the opposition, yet deadly in their finishing. Not bad for a foursome who'd soda jerked, parked cars and worked as salesmen, sharing a single auto in order to keep the group together. Perhaps it was all down to Clark Burroughs' cooking. Almost every night he'd concoct a casserole and then hand out vitamin pills in order that his fellow Hi-Los could both handle their day jobs and loosen their larynxes at night. But it paid off. First year out, the foursome shared just $5,000. One year later, they pulled in over $75,000.

Amazingly, the King Sisters, who'd been around since 1935, opted to become the female Hi-Los. And, though the odds seemed stacked against them, the Kings, whose real name was Driggs, successfully made the transition, cutting a Capitol album, *Imagination*, which remains the most harmonically advanced recording ever made by a girl group.

Most other vocal quartets set their sights at Freshmen level, which was more easily attained. Stan Kenton's Modern Men, the versatile Al Belletto Sextet, the Williams Brothers — all owed something to the Indianapolis-spawned foursome. And when the Beach Boys came surfing in from the west, it was just the Freshmen all over again, the sand-happy Brian

Bottom: *Lambert, Hendricks and Ross*
Left: *The Hi-Los*

Sing A Song of Basie

DAVE LAMBERT and his singers
JON HENDRICKS and his lyrics
featuring: ANNIE ROSS and the Basie Rhythm Section

JACKIE & ROY

Wilson and Co. paying tribute to their mentors on such recordings as 'Graduation Day', which the Freshmen had recorded many years earlier.

And though such groups as Manhattan Transfer these days attempt to emulate the sounds of harmony-singing's golden era, it's noticeable that, as yet, they've not attempted to revive memories of the Hi-Los and a vocal technique which one critic described as 'awesome'. Which figures.

51

CHICKS, CHIRPERS, CHARMERS ALL

They were shapely, decorous, wolf-whistle worthy. They all came poured into dresses that accentuated their superstructure. And when not rousing the ardour of the out-front punters, they contended with the more rigorous, attention-grabbing exploits of the musicians with whom they worked.

They also sang. Did it well, too. For they were the singers with the big bands of the thirties and forties – the misses with the mostest, the sweet and the all-reet. Every compere introduced them with a similar array of slick phrases, and most comperes, bless their hammy, hip-zip-hooray scripts, were damn right.

Life on the big-band road taught singers certain disciplines – how to handle arrangements that came sometimes corny, sometimes musically ambitious. And working alongside the best jazz musicmakers in the land also rubbed off. Sometimes it got so you couldn't tell the instrumental solo from what in those days was known as 'the vocal refrain'. If Lady sounded a lot like Lester and vice versa, then it was no surprise.

Many of the girls simply lived music. Home life often comprised just spending time with the musician with whom they'd just played a hundred or so gigs. Doris Day, of the Bob Crosby and Les Brown bands, first married trombonist Al Jorden before partnering saxman George Weidler; Woody Herman's Frances Wayne and Mary Ann McCall wedded arranger-trumpeter Neal Hefti and sax ace Al Cohn respectively; Stan Kenton got hitched to vocalist Ann Richards, while his best-known singer, June Christy, did the 'I do' bit with tenor saxist Bob Cooper. And there were scores of similar relationships.

They started young too. Day joined Crosby when she was sixteen. Kay Starr made it into the Glenn Miller band at seventeen; Lena Horne sang with Noble Sissle at eighteen; while Billie Holiday made her recording debut with Benny Goodman at a similar age. It was strictly teenage parade. By the time such singers were into their twenties they were veterans, ready to handle any charts tossed on to the stands, able to swop choruses with the greatest of *Downbeat* and *Metronome* instrumental poll-winners.

Certainly this was true in the case of Ella Fitzgerald. She sang with drummer Chick Webb's band for five years and when Webb died, it was she, rather than any of the star musicians, who was asked to front the aggregation. Fitzgerald has never possessed a particularly black voice. And she often sounds little-girlish, a trifle naive, in comparison with Holiday, Dinah Washington, Peggy Lee, Sarah Vaughan and other upper-echelon big-band graduates. But nobody has ever scatted in such razor-edge mode as Ella; nobody has ever vocally caught the spirit of Hamp's 'Air Mail Special' or 'Flying Home' in a way that could both remind you of, yet still make you forget, Illinois Jacquet. Perhaps, anyway, she was there first. Earbend to the final vocal chorus of Chick Webb's 1939 recording of 'Tain't What You Do' and hear Ella not only scat happily but also bow out on the word 'rebop'. A lady ahead of her time.

But if Ella is jazz's Ms Clean, then Anita O'Day, who helped spark the Gene Krupa and Stan Kenton bands, is the one most likely to be the subject of a bio-pic next time

Hollywood needs a subject in the style of *Lady Sings The Blues*. Brash and unmitigatedly jazzy, her voice acted as the fan to Roy Eldridge's trumpet flame while the twosome tried upstaging each other in front of the Krupa band. Later she joined Kenton and sounded so right that virtually all of the leader's later vocalists adopted a similar style. Whenever you hear June Christy or Chris Connor, you're hearing a little of Anita. But she latched on to the wrong sort of medical pick-me-ups, found guys who were pull-her-downs and eventually her story became more heroin than heroine, a fifteen-year habit ending in an OD that saw her being declared dead. She didn't die though. She came through and sang just as grittily as she'd done since the forties. If Ella Fitzgerald was black singing white, then O'Day reversed the process. A pity that dope addled her way.

The greatest white singer though? Those into sure things should place bets on Peggy Lee. Peg's the one person who can flip through a Holiday song and, while still reminding you of Billie, can manage to add something that's uniquely her own. She can cut the blues like the best of black singers and even read a poem in a manner that's soft, but not hickey. Even in her earliest days with Benny Goodman she phrased like a cool angel. Her vocal on Goodman's recording of 'Why Don't You Do Right', a Lee-penned song, made the single the sharpest on the block, the most potent non-black finger-snapper of 1942. When Peg eventually went solo, there were no fears for her survival. For the lady had talent to spare. She wrote hits, provided film scores, wrote poetry, painted and eventually turned into a classy actress. In 1957,

Capitol put a band together called Ten Cats And A Mouse – and the Mouse was Peg, pounding a drum kit behind a frontline that included such musicians as Benny Carter, 'Red' Norvo, Billy May and Bobby Sherwood. Dizzy Gilles-pie, once speculating on whom he'd place in government if given the chance, opted immediately for Peggy Lee as Ministress For Labour. Made sense. Cat knows every job in the book.

Peg, Billie, Anita, Ella, Betty Carter, Carmen McRae, Helen Humes, Lena Horne, Julie London, all paid their dues as 'canaries', glams with gams, some of the torchy, hopefully smouldering sex symbols that every big band leader toted around, as much as a decorative measure as that of a musical addition. That they all made it out of the wardrobe stakes and into an area where larynx meant more than lurex, says as much as anything about not only their undoubted musical talent but also their ability to survive in what was originally a man's, man's world.

Lena Horne

June Christy   _Sarah Vaughan_

Julie London

Billie Holiday

Jeri Southern

KITTENS
ON THE KEYS

Keyboard queens were right there at the starting gate whenever black music shimmied down a new course. Would Jump have jumped half as much without a subtle shove from Mary Lou Williams? Many believe not. When boogie became the rage during the mid-thirties Mary Lou wrote the big band boogie blueprint, 'Little Joe From Chicago' for Andy Kirk's Clouds Of Joy. Mary Lou later claimed that she regarded boogie and blues as kids' stuff and moved into bop where she remained the front-runner she'd always been. Boogie, though, provided the breakthrough for many of the keyboard kittens. Maybe the idea of a high-class gal highpowering it in some booze-cruise of a nightspot turned the men on. The nun in suspenders theory, maybe. Whatever the reason, such performers as Hazel Scott, Hadda Brooks, Cleo Brown, Dorothy Donegan and Rose Murphy high-tailed their way through an eight-to-the-bar repertoire during the forties and did their bank-balances no harm at all.

But no matter how hard they pounded, however gritty the lyrics might be, they maintained the keyboard chic image, dressed in gowns that would have been razzle-dazzlers at a President's inauguration ball. Some came on raunchier – but still got invitations on White House note paper. Kansas City's Julia Lee – composer of such double-entendre specials as 'Snatch And Grab It' and 'All This Beef And Ripe Tomatoes' made it out of the gin-mill to play Harry

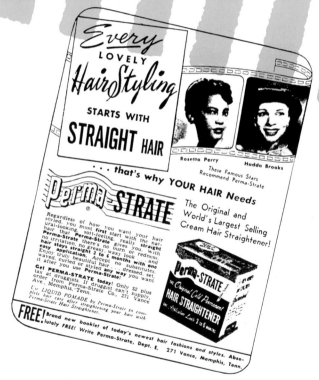

Truman's inaugural shindig. Innovative and ever ready to jump, Lee nudged black music into the realms of rock. She had but one real rival – Capitol stablemate, Nellie Lutcher, who bopped along similar salacious rails. Nobody, but nobody, had a sound like Lutcher, handling lyrics as though she was translating them into another language – even coming up with an item called, 'The Pig Latin Song'.

As rock moved in, the cocktail sock-it-to-'em sophisticates were elbowed into other occupations and the riff-rippling women at the piano faded from the mainstream of music. Yet, nowadays, there are those who maintain the tradition – Nina Simone remains as proof that power can be just one pair of hands and a voice steeped in emotion, while Blossom Dearie says it for those who like their jazz pretty and witty. Aretha (when she ditches disco to rock steady at the Steinway), along with Roberta Flack, Shirley Horn and Barbara Carroll all reflect one aspect or another of the often not-so-gentle art of kitten on the keys.

Hazel Scott

HARLEM HOOFERS

Dance has always been part of jazz, from the Delta shuffle up to the urban tantrum of tap and into the body-poppin' breakdancers of the South Bronx and Michael Jackson's thriller-diller video. The most famous hoofer in history, Fred Astaire, has always acknowledged his debt to tap dancers like Bill 'Bojangles' Robinson. Sets of shoes of both these dancers repose in glass display cabinets in New York's famed Roseland Ballroom.

The golden age of tap was the Big Band era – a time when Basie, Ellington and Herman would give just as much prominence to speed-tappers like Baby Laurence and Bunny Briggs as they did to their featured vocalists. You can still get a glimpse of the art in movies like *Stormy Weather*, with Bill Robinson and the Nicholas Brothers.

'Tap dancing', Baby Laurence insisted, 'is very much like jazz music. The dancer improvises his own solo and expresses himself.'

Jazz tap derives from drum techniques. The heel is the bass drum, and keeps time. The toes play the melody. The side of the foot plays cymbals, and the ball of the foot is the tom-tom. Tap dancers can play paradiddles, launch rim-shots and deliver a sock-beat. The four steel taps on the soles of the shoes are tuned like the strings of the banjo. Indeed, when he was a Luis Russell Orchestra sideman, an ebullient Dizzy Gillespie would often play frantic 'chase' choruses with guest hoofers.

The art of the dance passed through the great King 'Rastus' Brown (from whom Bojangles lifted his now famous up-and-down stairs routine), Buck and Bubbles (Ford Lee Washington and John Sublett), Bill Bailey, Teddy Hales, Honi Coles, the super-stylish Eddie Rector, Slappy Wallace, Rubberlegs Williams, James Barton (another Bojang-

les mentor), Earl 'Snakehips' Tucker, Derby Wilson, Bunny Briggs, Will Gaines, Sammy Davis Jr and the man often likened to both Bird and 'Trane – Baby Laurence.

There were also the teams – The Nicholas Brothers (Fayard and Harold) and 'flash act' fanatics, the Berry Brothers, a thrills-and-spills threesome who specialized in acrobatics as opposed to tap. When, in 1937, both acts shared the same Cotton Club Revue stage, they virtually crippled themselves in their efforts to upstage one another.

Jazz tap almost died out until Chuck Green was rediscovered in the late sixties. Chuck, boosted by a documentary film *No Maps On My Taps* (which also features Lionel Hampton), formed the Harlem Hoofers Club and started touring. In the age of rock 'n' roll, the square world had slept on jazz tap. Now it woke up...

Dance was back.

Chuck Green 'If you wanna keep a nickel, put a buffalo on it.'

Sandman Sims 'What Chuck means is that he put a buffalo on the floor. You can't go behind that. It means he's bad. He's really doin' it! When he gets through dancing, you wouldn't put nothing on that spot but a leopard!'

Sandman Sims 'It was in New York where tap really was. Baby Laurence, Teddy Hale, Teddy Kelly, Groundhog. We'd go looking for each other. We'd dance on the street, anywhere we met. When I first got hip to street dancing, I saw Chuck Green and California Jack Williams dance all night and all day and half the next night, and they had to shake hands and go away. They was dancing in their sneakers on

Far left: *Astaire*
Below: *Bojangles*
Left: *The Nicholas Brothers*

59

the sidewalk.

'They run us underground. I got picked up by the police and put in jail for a week for dancing on the streets at night, disturbing the peace. The judge asked, he said, what was I doing at twelve o'clock at night? I said, I was dancing. He said, what do you mean? I danced in front of him. He said, you mean to tell me this is what they picked you up for? Case dismissed. We had to dance and run.

'When the big bands died, that killed it because most of them carried a tap dancer. I did close to ten years with Lionel Hampton. I hadn't never been on a stage before. My first professional job was with him at the Golden Gate Theatre in San Francisco. I got on the stage and I danced with my back to the audience because I was watching the music. Everybody in the band was shouting "TURN ROUND!" I kept turning round and round and round. I made about thirty turns. I didn't know they meant face the audience. They got so tickled that I didn't know when to quit.

'I started out as a lightweight boxer, but I found the crowd, they preferred what I did in the rosin box between rounds to my fighting. So I quit and started dancing in a sand-tray. When I challenged someone on the street in New York, the minute I got to doing the sand, they quit. They'd give up, man. Guy'd come round, "Hey – let's look for Sandman." They say, "No, man – he gonna *sand* on us! We don't want that. Outlaw that. That's taboo!" I useta get a lotta TKOs because when it got real tough, I'd put that sand on them. Bill Robinson told me to hang on to my novelty because his dancing up-and-down the stairs had kept him working. Well, mine kept me working all the time the rock 'n' roll was blasting, when tap dancers was twenty cents a dozen. The bookers'd tell me, you come without that sand, boy, you stay home.

'I'd put my shoes on and have sessions with different drummers – Art Blakey, Max Roach, Philly Joe Jones and Lionel Hampton. But the one that really put my boots on was Big Sid Catlett. We useta brush all day long. Oh, he'd brush me to death, man! Nobody'd bother me in the sand when they found I could keep up with him.'

Babs Gonzales 'Baby Laurence is a symphony in dancing. He is also a very slick cat. Him and Charlie Parker burned more people than anybody I ever met. In the early fifties he and Teddy Hale used to have cutting sessions at the Heat Wave on 145th Street and 8th Avenue. The boss used to pay me forty to find Baby at noon, keep him with me all day to make sure he showed up.

'Another incident involved Baby on his first gig at Newport. He was up there and didn't have no stuff. Eric Dolphy was out practising by the sea, so Baby stole his wallet with $75 and car keys. He set out for New York to cop and got as far as Providence, where he wrecked the car. The promoter came and got him out and the police cut him loose soon as he danced in the joint.'

Chet Baker 'One prison I was in, there was Baby Laurence. He used to use his entire exercise period on the yard to tap dance. He'd dance up the walls, man.'

Babs Gonzales (talking about Rubberlegs Williams) 'Rubber was queer, but he weighed 240 and could whip any two cats easy. If he saw a cat he wanted, it was no problem, 'cause if the dude didn't give it up peacefully, he would just whip his ass and take it. Everytime he hit on me I would just say, "Miss Rubber, I need five for my room rent", and he'd just say, "Go 'head Miss Thing, I ain't got no money." In his last years he was a cook uptown and all the hungry cats could eat daily when rigor mortis was on them.'

Clayton 'Peg-leg' Bates 'I'm Peg-Leg Bates, that one-legged dancing fool. I own thirteen peg-legs, one to fit every suit, all colours...'

60

REVEL WITHOUT A PAUSE,
OR
HOOTING WITH THE HIP

Music apart, jazz spawned a corresponding slipstream of verbal language that mocked, knocked and melted meaning into comical new shapes. Jazzmen had evolved their own slang which walled off the square world, but with the emergence of bebop in the forties, a small coterie of hipsters began marketing stand-up presentations of the rap itself.

The adrenalin energy of bebop was uncontainable. It was so chock-a-block with stuttering sidesteps and scissor-leaps that the audience found itself gnashing the knees and popping the fingers like flints to burn off some of the excess rhythmic fuel. Singers gave wordless shape to the energy itself, oo-bop-sh'bamming syllables from the flip-top of the flapping wig. Anybody hip tried to paste the tongue against that live cable and FLASH! Cats scatted words to saxophone solos or, like Kerouac, tried to plug the written line into 'Now's The Time'. Funniest in this gibberish Dervish Derby were Slim Gaillard, Leo Watson, Babs Gonzales and Harry 'The Hipster' Gibson. Best of the bunch, neither black nor musician, was Lord Buckley.

Born Richard Buckley around the turn of the century in California, part Indian, Buckley's routine goes back to prohibition's Chicago speakeasies in the twenties. The details of his life are conjectural. It is said that he ennobled himself, robing in the trappings of a circus elephant, led sixteen naked citizens through the lobby of the Royal Hawaiian Hotel, and set up his own Church of the Living Swing to showcase his sermons, a brace of belly-dancers flanking the pulpit, the new religion promptly disestablished when the Vice Squad screened the scene. Like Sun Ra, Lord Buckley held court, and then some.

It wasn't until the rise of long-playing records, *Evergreen Review*, City Lights Bookshop, Grove Press and the Beats that the smart set dug it had slept on Lord Buckley – and rushed to mis-file him with the anti-Ike improvising satirists like Mort Sahl.

Admittedly, Buckley isn't easy to classify. The pith helmet and waxed Dali moustache are vaudeville's version of the rulers of the Raj, while the squashy transcendentalist philosophy blows a soapbubble towards the hippy era. The pipes, like those of the later Tom Waits, take a hit off Satchmo, but the delivery is actor-manager's ham. The high hip semantic is jazz. The comedy comes from a cartoonist's imagination in which single-characteristic responses govern all human behaviour. 'Rhythm is the key to everything,'

61

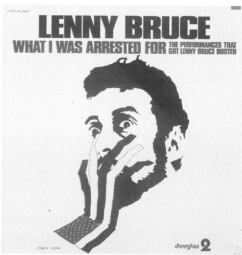

Buckley proclaimed, 'runs the whole swingin' thing!' It certainly tied an improbable parcel for him.

His best-known routines are preposterously inflated jive eulogies to the famous. 'You gotta be a reincarnation cat like myself, you gotta RE-dig and RE-call the ball.' BC or AD, Buckley's ball was uniformly post-Minton's, and starred a cavalcade of cats like Jesus, de Sade, James Dean, Nero, Gandhi and Shakespeare, all goofin' on down the boulevard together.

'The Naz' is a recommendation of The Nazarene, Jesus Christ. At a stroke, Buckley cuts through all New English, nouvelle cuisine, cork-tipped, non-gosh interpretation to put his Naz back on the spangled stand, dishing miracle licks and mysterioso like the barker of a sideshow.

'I'm gonna put a cat on you who was the sweetest, grooviest, strongest, wailingest, swingingest, most far-out cat that ever stomped on this jumpin' green sphere, and they called this here cat . . . THE NAZ!' Pausing only to recruit the twelve apostles – 'Wait a minute, babies, tell ya what I'm gonna do. Ain't gonna take two, four, six, eight of you cats, I'm gonna take ALL TWELVE of you studs and straighten you all at the same time. You look pretty hip, you buddy with me' – the Naz was up and running, straightening cats with bent frames, knocking the corners off the squares, running the money-changers outa the temple on a rail, putting The Word on the cats, like Dig And Thou Shalt Be Dug and Drag Not And Thou Shalt Not Be Drug.

The Feeding of the Five Thousand features one of Buckley's lung-bursting chin-music cadenzas. 'The Naz is a-talkin' and a-swingin' with how pretty the hour, how pretty the flower, how pretty you, how pretty she, how pretty the tree – Naz had them pretty eyes, wanted ever'body to see to pin the golden rosette of reality – and they is havin' such a wailin', swingin', glorianna style stompin' hike that before you know it, it was scoffin' time and these poor cats is forty miles outa town, ain't nobody got the first biscuit! "We wuz diggin' so hard what you wuz puttin' down, Naz, we didn't PRE-pare. We goofed!"'

From the Sweet Double Hipness of the Holy Land, Lord Buckley turns his supercharged historical shovel on William 'Willie The Shake' Shakespeare. 'They gave this cat five cents-worth of ink and a nickel's-worth of paper, and he sat down and wrote up such a breeze – WHAM! – that's all there was, Jack! There was NO MORE! Ever'body got off. Pen in hand, he was a Mutha Superior.' Samples of the Bard's cooking include a greasy version of the funeral oration from

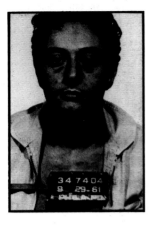

The Buckley beat was a prime influence on comedian Lenny Bruce, but for his material Lenny turned over a different stone. Maybe he was born under it. This wasn't the wig-bubble extravaganza blown by Buckley's peace-pipe so much as a back-up by the toilet. His mother, professionally known as Boots Malloy, was a burlesque comic who also trained strippers. It was a far cry from the squashy sentimentality of 'Born in a Trunk'. Baby Lenny's crib attendants were drawn from a cast of pimps, hookers, hustlers, pushers and the cheaper chisellers. Coming up, he worked the G-string joints where the girls whirled the tassels on their tits and the tenorman rammed a knee into the bell of the saxophone to burp up the low B-flat. He was raised in the armpit of entertainment, and it conditioned his view of the world. Everything was shtick.

Lenny had it in for everything, and bugged across the board. No section of society escaped his lashing, scatological broadside. America's moral values, the family, democracy, religion, toleration, justice, were indistinguishable from the spit, sawdust and smut of a bump 'n' grind burlesque parlour.

'Religions Inc.', one of his recorded routines, features a top-level inter-denominational brainstormer on Madison Avenue. 'For the first time in twelve years Catholicism is up nine points, Judaism is up fifteen, and The Big P, Pentecostal, is starting to move finally.' Like Lord Buckley, Lenny has a wicked ear for voices, and is extraordinarily nippy at creating a cast. 'Let's make the scene together because if we burn each other, where are we gonna end up, you dig?' It is ecumenicity as show-biz merger, the whole tacky tamale only momentarily interrupted by a phone call from the Pope. 'What's shakin', baby? I can getcha the Sullivan Show the nineteenth. Wear the big ring. The ratings? We can fix that!'

Other routines featured the president considering a strategic cabinet assassination or two to recruit sympathy for the Administration – 'But some of these things backfire, you know?'; and a gathering of the medical professional to settle on a money-spinner – 'We can get even with a new disease. In Lenny's world, all principles are a put-on, functioning solely in terms of marquee value for the credulous schmuck in the street. In private, all public figures pinch each others'

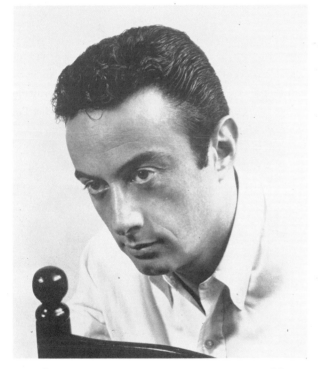

Julius Caesar that opens with 'Hipsters, flipsters and finger-poppin' daddies/Knock me your lobes', and concludes movingly with 'Dig me hard, my ticker is there in the coffin with Caesar/And yea, I must stay cool 'til it flippeth back to me.'

Both Buckley and Babs Gonzales re-dug Lincoln's Gettysburg address. 'All cats and kitties, red, white or blue, are created level, in front', roared the leapin' Lord, underlining America's lapses from the guarantee. 'Four C's of black and white ago', sneered Babs, 'some dude eased into this crib with a jive story that all men were created equal.'

Solid.

In the words of Henry Miller, a fan, 'It is very far out, your Lordship. . .'

cheeks, call each other sweetie, and carry on like vaudeville agents.

Where Buckley ranted in rhythm, Lenny glided like a snake. There is a hipster's indifference in his delivery, whether purring faggishly or huffily pouting over some homespun homily. He is a master of mimicry and accent, a repository of every all-American sentimental-as-a-locket cinema cliché. Given the power, he would have re-cast Norman Rockwell's covers for catamites and given the Henry Fonda parts to a coprophiliac, non-union member.

Whether he stood for the healing lancet or Swiftian satire or strictly for Lenny, the square world was not slow to sense the threat and get his ass in the wringer. Chicago condemned his night-club act on grounds of immorality – they counted the 'fucks' – and indicted him for obscenity, while on the West Coast he was hounded for narcotics. The British home secretary had him deported from a season at The Establishment – 'Prince Charles is really a forty year-old midget' – and his last years were obsessed with his various lawsuits. By the time he died in 1966, the process of canonization was already under way. The young Lenny would have sneered at the idea of Lenny the Martyr; the sad, blown junkie might have settled.

The hipster started out in black urban America as a reaction to living in a white world. What might have looked like paranoia in Lenny Bruce's rap, was the plain fact of persecution in the everyday black reality. For survival's sake, the hipster disengaged, not even leaving the ringing-tone. Not until Dick Gregory resolved in the sixties to be 'a coloured funny man, not a funny coloured man' did black comics break out of the insulting stereotypes – the illiterate lazybones, the eye-rolling Pullman porter, the Aunt Jemima bent on negro heaven in which God smoked five-cent cigars.

Rochester and Amos 'n' Andy and Buckwheat must've spun in their graves with the appearance of Richard Pryor. He didn't tell take-away gags, and he held a mirror up to the floor of America. Like Lord Buckley and Lenny Bruce, he ran his improvisation on reflexes, head just ahead of the overdrive. In the mid-sixties, safe and successful enough to appear on the Ed Sullivan and Johnny Carson shows, he suddenly quit in the middle of a Las Vegas performance. 'It stopped being fun, you know. I was doin' that safe kinda shit, and it was hollow. "Good evening, ladies and gentlemen – I was only kidding, hahaha – I'm putting my cock back in. No offence, but wasn't it cute?" That kinda thing. No matter what you did, you always had to clean up. I quit.' He moved on to the hipster's turf, fast, impatient, off the top of the wig, shaping the rap against the response. His themes were the blues themes, and they drove straight at the heart of the ghetto – wounds recognized, the same bind, comic and community on the same hook and hanging together. He worked in snatched adrenalin playlets, the pain out front: low wages, job treadmill, the weekly release of a Saturday night on the town, but . . . 'The cops put a hurtin' on your ass, you know. Whites know them like, "Hello Officer Timson – going bowling tonight? My licence? Glad to be of help." Niggers don't know them like that. "I am reachin' in my pocket fo' my licence." "Get outta the car, take your pants down, spread your cheeks. There's been a robbery, nigger looked just like you." Just go home, baby, beat ya kids. Take that shit out on somebody.'

Pryor deals in jive talk, since black Americans are the only minority without their own language. He uses a narrow vocabulary with a range of nuance so wide that meaning resides in the fall of italics. Obscenity has no meaning in a ghetto world where 'ass' is the fundament of selfhood – 'Death was quite a surprise to his ass' – and 'muthafucker' the small-change of social greeting. Life and language are on iron rations, with no room for the luxury of liberalism or the bijouterie of radical chic.

Pryor, like most professional comics, isn't privately a barrel of laffs. 'Get to your own peace, that's the thing. It's hard to keep it though, man, because – shit! – you gotta eat. I mean that's how they gotcha. You gotta go out there and eat, that's the fuckin' trick. You can wake up feelin' great, but you're gonna say hello to those muthafuckers sometime during the day.' Hollywood hasn't helped, snapping him up, only to squander his brilliance in wheel-clamped vehicles. Still, despite what Tinsel Town did for Lady Day, hopes are riding on the promised Pryor casting for *The Life Of Charlie Parker*. He's been playing *that* part all his life.

If Richard Pryor has left black comedians with a blank cheque on the Bank of Funland, young Eddie Murphy has been the first to cash it. A millionaire at twenty-two, he seems to have sidestepped the struggles. He has risen with the speed of a rock star, vaulting from Manhattan's showcase, 'The Comic Strip', to NBC's 'Saturday Night Live', and from there to the boffo box-office movies, *48 Hours*, *Trading Places* and *Beverly Hills Cop*.

Like Pryor, he is not the whites' idea of a credit to his race: 'Old people that get offended easily – get the fuck out now!' is one of his openers. 'Also faggots aren't allowed to look at my ass while I'm on stage. That's why I keep moving. I do some nasty shit while I'm up here.' He does, too, a decreasing proportion of it falling into the hip bag. He learned his world from TV, sitting at home in a Long Island suburb, and can snap between media impersonations with the speed of a channel-flicker. Still, if product assimilates him, he has still left a few definitive portrayals of the jive-ass-mutha-fucker on film as a legacy.

The hardest-wearing vintage GI surplus has to be Phil Silvers' 'Sergeant Bilko' series on TV. It's still as wrinkle-free as it was when it first appeared in 1955 under the title 'You'll Never Get Rich'. It ran for four years in 144 episodes, taking five Emmy awards on the try-out. The series made Phil Silvers a star, and he never rose higher or revved faster. Like Cagney, he uses up all available oxygen, leaving the rest of the cast to gasp and flounder. 'But Sarge . . .' must be the busiest line in the script.

TV – a rag-bag medium in the mid-fifties – tapped the tradition of burlesque and vaudeville and flushed out Phil Silvers who had established a corner in street-smart hust- lers. Top comedy writer Nat Hiken devised the Fort Baxter format with Silvers as Bilko, and the hunt was on for comic faces. Duane Doberman (Maurice Gosfield) was snapped up for his natural ineptitude with a line and impressive slob- bishness. Colonel Hall (Paul Ford) was drafted in through a fortunate resemblance to a basset hound. The rest of Fort Baxter's dog-faces came courtesy of casting director, Rocky Graziano, who had a soft spot for old sparring partners.

With its all-canine cartoon cast, there is never any doubt about the top dog. Silvers surfboards on his own rearing adrenalin – and the breakdowns, divorces, hypochondria and gambling fevers that are documented in his autobiography are the price. Time and again the screen composes into a chevron with Bilko at the apex. All information proceeds from him, and the squad leans close to his brain, eavesdropping in droves. Bilko is always on, orchestrating all responses. No one is secure from his raffles, while around the card table his fellow sergeants, sharp as bolsters, are regularly four-flushed into the red.

Despite flat lighting, utility sets, scurrying music and a cast who resemble rejects from Crufts, 'Sergeant Bilko' remains the hippest comedy show ever to hit the box.

BA'AD ATTITUDE

Tony Scott 'Duke Ellington and his band, it was like being around a man and wife who're always nagging at each other but stay together. They owed him and he owed them, and they couldn't really settle the bill.

'I got in an argument on the bus with Mingus one time. He says, "You white people are always telling us how to talk." I turned round and said, "I'm darker than you are, Mingus." Mingus is about my colour. I'm a Sicilian, and he had a lotta white blood in there. He was trying to prove he was a black man and I took his negritude away. He came up behind me – I had bebop glasses on – and strangled me, one hand around my throat and one over my eyes. Britt Woodman and Clark Terry pulled him off. Britt wouldn't look at him after that, and Mingus said, "Man, I must've stepped on my dick. My best friend won't look at me."

'I was there when Mingus had that big to-do with Juan Tizol: Juan with a machete, Mingus with a fire-axe. Duke had to fire him. Duke said to Mingus, "Look – Juan Tizol is an old problem. Why don't you resign? You're a new problem."'

Buddy Tate 'Basie hired Don Byas. Don pulled a stunt one night, got drunk and pulled a pistol on the band. Ben Webster was working on 52nd Street and he came in and Basie asked Don to get down and let Ben play some. All the guys raved over Ben that night, and Don got drunk and went out and came back with a piece. I didn't drink then and Don always used to say to me, "Now look – I know we're friends and if ever my slip is showing, you tell me." So that night Basie tells me to talk to him, and I walk over to him. He says, "Get back over there with them!" I says OK. I go back over there too. The valet got a house policeman and they got up behind him and grabbed him, took the gun, and the valet carried him home. Next day, Basie gave him his two weeks' notice and the valet carried it up to him. He's still drunk in the bed. The valet says, "Here's your money." Byas says, "Goddamn – about time they gave me a raise." The valet says, "Gave you a raise? They raised you out of the band!"'

Billy Eckstine 'We were in a little jazz joint in Chicago. God rest his soul, Trane was alive then. He would sometimes get very boring, take a very slow ballad and do chorus one thousand eight hundred and fifty on it. Trane has gone through all this, and he's played all he's gonna play in the first two choruses. Little Jimmy Heath leans over to me, he says, "B – Trane's blowin' right on past the money, ain't he."'

Babs Gonzales (On Charlie Parker pawning two of Babs' zoot suits after staying at his pad.)
'Bird handed me the tickets, and said, "Babs, my man, the threads are in for ten apiece. Here's a twenty to bail them out, and a dime for your trouble."'

Bobby Hutcherson 'One time I was staying in this guy's house in New York on 22nd Street. We had this old piano, just the soundboard with all the strings on it and it was pulling apart every day from the heat of New York. We were gonna hafta take it and throw it away. We lived up on the fourth floor and there was a concrete patio below, so I said, "WAIT A MINUTE! Let's go down and put a tape recorder down there, throw it out the window and hear what this shit's gonna sound like. I mean, you're gonna get to hear all eighty-eight notes on the piano AT ONCE – and when it hits, this has gotta be THE BADDEST CHORD there is!" So we got it up in the window and called one of these drunks off the street to give it the final push. We're down there on the ground with the tape recorder – and HERE IT COMES, man!

'It's coming down and it starts singing because the wind is coming through the wires, like WHEEEE, all these beautiful chords, real light – and then WHAAAAHOOOOM! And, man, this chord hits and it's just like someone flipped a switch on from darkness to light! It just stayed there and swelled like an atomic bomb.'

That Max Roach Quintet Concert at Graz, Austria, 1963

Ronnie Matthews 'Oh really? WOW! A record came out?'

Freddie Hubbard 'They recorded THAT? Listen, is my speech in there? About Hitler being a faggot, and some stuff about the Gestapo? Well, I got it off my chest. I was drunk. Here's how it happened, man. The whole tour was a bummer anyway. We had a four-hour plane ride, then a four-hour bus through the Austrian Alps to Graz. Ice on each side and thousands of feet drop. You miss a turn, man, you're dead. I turned to the driver and said I thought he was going a bit fast for the road conditions. He shrugged, so I began drinking beer. By the time I got to the concert I was drunk.

'The promoter made us go straight on, wouldn't let me sit down for a moment and get my breath, so that infuriated me. I didn't think the audience understood English. They almost lynched me, man.'

Ronnie Matthews 'We were rushed off the stage locked in the dressing room, and finally chained up by the Austrian police. In the cells, we just stood there with our mouths open. We looked out of the window and there was a lynch mob. There's no other word for it. All these angry faces and shaken fists. I wondered if I was gonna get home alive.'
(Max Roach bailed them out, 350 dollars apiece, and the band were conducted to the airport by the police.)

Johnny Griffin 'Tubby Hayes? That was my buddy! Tubby Hayes and Jimmy Deuchar. Why, they put us out of all the nice towns in Switzerland. Yeah, the Dirty Trio. Every place we'd be, it'd end up being a riot. I imagine we were pretty out-of-hand because everybody loved the booze. Talk loud, laugh a little too loudly, disturb all the elderly hotel guests in the rich resort areas. We'd get nice escorts all the way to the train station. They'd pack our bags and take us right to the train.'

Babs Gonzales 'One night while packing to leave St Louis a cat asked me could he ride up to Chicago with me. He was going up to cop, dig? I charged him ten beans and when we got to Chi, we checked in at John Williams hotel on 47th Street. We went up to Miles room and there was his brother Vernon and a cat named Moss. The set up was for the cat to give the $300 to Moss to cop. Moss was supposed to burn the dude and later on split with Miles and Vernon. The cat laid his bread on Moss who cut out. The fool waited three days in Chi before he realized he'd been burned.

'Now Miles and Vernon is looking for Moss as the rent is due. They couldn't find him nowhere. About a week later out on 63rd Street I ran into Moss. He was sharp, new suit, shoes and had his white whore on his arm. He said, "Gonzi, Miles and Vernon were trying to use me so I burned both chumps. Here's ten to put in your slide and if they ask you, you ain't seen me, dig?" I said "Cool . . ."'

Johnny Griffin 'I always had this competition with Art Blakey, front line against the rhythm section, so it was WAR! I was working six days a week with Thelonious and Monday nights in Birdland with Philly Joe, Wilbur Ware and Red Garland, like that. This was Labor Day, the first day I'd had off, so I was gonna repair my body a little, not gonna drink, just gonna relax.

'Well, I went by Art Blakey's house and got into an

argument. He started talking about the drums, and I said, who needs drums making all that noise, I play my saxophone, I don't need no drums. We started drinking of course, friendly conversation but getting loud. Babs Gonzales comes in, and he starts adding a little spice to it to get us going and we ended up making a fifty dollar bet.

'The Baroness, Nica von Koenigswarter Rothschild, called up to know what was going on, so we said we had this bet and we were going uptown to 155th Street in Harlem to this joint, and Art Blakey was gonna make me spit blood or I was gonna make him throw away his drumsticks. She came by and picked us up in her convertible Bentley – Babs, Art Blakey and myself – and we go in the club. Ram Ramirez, the man who wrote "Loverman", he's in there with his organ trio. He's got his nice programme going... and here come the maniacs! He says, "Oh – a jam session with the organ!" We tell him we don't want no organ. Just the saxophone and the drums. We get up on stage and start blowing, both of us out of our minds.

'A stick slips out of Art Blakey's hand! And I say, "I WIN THE FIFTY DOLLARS!" No no no no no! I gotta fight him now to get the fifty dollars. OK – it was a slip. So we go on blowing until Ram's gotta go back on.

'We decide to go by Count Basie's. That's a good place to go. Good crowd. Lockjaw's working there with Shirley Scott, so when they see me with my horn, they say, "Oh – we're gonna have a tenor battle! Griffin and Lock!" I'm not thinking about Lock at this time, all I'm thinking about is beating Art Blakey out of his fifty dollars. So we start playing. But right to this day I don't know what happened to that fifty dollars, don't remember how the evening ended. It's all a haze. All I remember is that the next day I was trembling so much I had to have a drink because I was playing with Monk at the Five Spot.'

Philly Joe Jones

The great hard bop drummer, Philly Joe Jones, lived for a while in London, supporting himself by giving drum tuition to forty students a week. Lessons were £2 an hour. Keith Moon, the drummer with The Who, dropped in to pick up a few pointers. Philly Joe pointed at the trap set. 'Show me whatcha can do.' Moon pulled out a pair of drumsticks the size of truncheons, and battered the kit for ten minutes.

'So, how much did you say you earned a week doin' *that*?' asked Philly Joe. The answer was in thousands. 'Well – I really don't wanna spoil it for ya', said the tutor.

Quincy Jones 'I remember playing with Lionel Hampton – who was really the first rock and roll bandleader, even though he had a jazz background – and we were at the Bandbox in New York. Clifford Brown, Art Farmer and I were in the trumpet section. We had to wear Bermuda shorts, purple jackets and Tyrolian hats and when we played "Flying Home", Hamp marched the band outside. I was nineteen years old, so hip it was painful, and didn't want to know about anything that was close to being commercial.

'So Hamp would be in front of the sax section, and beating his drum sticks all over the awning, and soon he'd have most of the band behind him. But Brownie and I would stop to tie our shoes or do something so we wouldn't have to go outside, because next door was Birdland and there was Monk and Dizzy and Bud Powell, all the bebop idols standing in front at intermission saying, "What is this shit?"'

Hampton Hawes

While army bound in Japan, pianist Hampton Hawes was approached by local female keyboard-player Toshiko Akiyoshi who asked: 'How do you play the blues that way? How can I learn to play so authentically?' To which Hawes replied: 'I play the blues right because I eat collard greens, black-eyed peas and corn pone and clabber.'

'Then where,' asked Akiyoshi ingenuously, 'can I get such food?'

Serge Chaloff

Baritone saxman Serge Chaloff was a mixed blessing in Woody Herman's second Herd. An incomparable musician, he was also the band's pusher and Woody was always on the point of firing him. On one occasion Chaloff forestalled him by throwing all the baritone parts, which he knew by heart, in the river. Usually, he would plead innocence. 'Hey! Woody, Baby, I'm straight, man. I'm clean.'

After one particularly sloppy gig, with half the Herd on the nod, Woody had a row on the bandstand with the main contagion, and then, getting nowhere went off to a bar. The joint was hot and crowded and Woody had finally got served, when he heard Chaloff in his ear.

'Hey! Woody, Baby, what do you wanna talk to me like that for? I'm straight, Baby, I'm straight.' Woody snapped. In the crowd, he unzipped and pissed down Chaloff's leg.

Joe Maini

Blowing alto in the Parker tradition was only one of Joe Maini's accomplishments. As Lenny Bruce's Rabelaisian sidekick, Maini gained notoriety on the Hollywood club scene for such pranks as on-stage flashing.

Now, commercial endorsement has always proved a profitable perk for a money-tight musician – a means of legitimately heisting a new axe and filling the wallet. One day, during a Selmer sax ad shoot, the well-blessed Maini –

bored with all the waiting around – mischievously slipped his schlong out and draped it on the bell of his shiny new Selmer.

Due to the atmospheric half-light, the photographer didn't detect anything unusual through the viewfinder, and neither did Selmer, which reproduced Maini's photograph in all the trade glossies. Maini's 'fans' had keener eyes, promptly transforming the mad-cap saxist into a much-envied bandroom pin-up!

Bud Powell

Bud Powell strolled into a Left Bank bar just in time to see the resident alcoholic pour down a drink, overturn the table and collapse in a stupor on the floor.

Said Bud, turning to the barman: 'I'll have one of those!'

Maynard Ferguson

In the middle of a number, Maynard Ferguson's lead alto, Jimmy Ford, signals to the baritone saxman that he needs a reed. Despite the fact that a baritone reed won't be much use to an alto, the baritone player slides off the concert stage, to the dressing room, returning with a brand new spare reed, and passes it along the horn section. At the next interval, Jimmy Ford reaches under his chair, comes up with a tub of ice cream, and digs in with the reed.

Phil Seaman

The *enfant terrible* of British hard bop, Phil Seaman took over the drum chair with the London production of *West Side Story* – a task he likened to 'towing the Queen Mary through a sea of Mars bars!'

Having nodded out during a performance, and having missed a cue no less than twice, Seaman suddenly awoke with a start, jumped to his feet, draped a sweat-soaked towel over an arm, thrashed a Turkish gong with all his might and, to a stunned theatre, announced from the orchestra pit: 'Dinner is served!' The audience and cast alike broke up.

On another occasion, a group of foreign dignitaries, seated in the front row of the stalls were visibly unmoved by the exciting song and dance spectacular. During the second half, Seaman climbed out from behind his kit, strolled up to the stone-faced visitors and made it known to everyone within earshot: 'Dunno 'bout you mate, but I'm havin' a fuckin' good time!'

Chaloff and Herman

THE MILES DAVIS DYNASTY

Miles Dewey Davis III has been jazz's embodiment of Hip for the past three decades. As a catalyst and star-maker, Miles is without peer. Through Miles' patronage, John Coltrane, Bill Evans, Cannonball Adderley, Herbie Hancock, Chick Corea, Keith Jarrett, Wayne Shorter, Joe Zawinul, George Benson, John McLaughlin, Tony Williams and Billy Cobham gained the widest exposure. Few of them quite knew how they found themselves on Miles' team. Stealthy, unpredictable, vain, charismatic, cryptic and contemptuous, Miles thrives in the shadows, poaches from his palatinate, and what he wants he takes.

Weather Report Roadie 'I was his road manager for two-and-a-half years and I never even got to understand his hand signals.'

Joe Zawinul 'I went to Miles' house one time and I played his piano. He was hiding behind things, sculptures and things. He's like a kid sometimes. Three or four months later he called me at two in the morning and told me to come to the studio at once, we have a session. Two minutes later he called back – "And bring that tune." The tune was "In A Silent Way".'

John McLaughlin 'I said, "Do you want all the chords?" He said "Yeah." I said, "That's gonna take some time." He said, "Is that a fact?"'

Art Blakey 'Miles tells it exactly like it is. Guys come up to Miles, hugging him. "Hey Miles – hey baby, gonna give me a gig?" And Miles says, "Doin' what?"'

Wayne Shorter I'd be playing at Birdland with Art Blakey, and Lee Morgan would say, "Miles is here." I'd say where? "In that corner. You won't see him. Miles is checkin' Shorter out." Lee was always starting things. He says that loud so Art could hear, and nod his head like "I know what's happenin." Finally, the lawyer phoned me and asked if I'd like to join the Miles Davis Organization. Harold Lovett – high-talkin' lawyer. He and Miles were two of the baddest dressers in New York. I wanted to . . . but I'd have left Art in trouble. Everywhere I played, there'd be Harold Lovett in the shadows, and "You must be CRAAAZY! The door's wide open." So, here's Miles on the phone. "I wanna hear some of your music. How about tonight. I'll be home." I went to his house with some music. J.J. Johnson was there, Cannonball. He had a big case of Scotch in the corner. I said "The stage is set!" So I sat at the piano and played "Children of the Night" and Miles came over and looked at the music. "Uh-huh." That was it.

'A month later Tony Williams and Herbie Hancock phoned me up and said, "There's a big hole in this band and you can fill it. C'mon, man!"

'Miles speaks in morse code. One time he had all the drummers lined up in his house, Billy Cobham, Lennie White, Jack DeJohnette. The only one to play was Jack. So Lennie asks about his turn, and Miles just tore him down by saying, "Jack, you done, you muthafucker?" All the drummers just waiting there, thinking like that's a helluva compliment, maybe I won't play at all.'

Chick Corea 'His approach wasn't unlike what you might call the early drug bebop approach. Let everything happen, man. It's all very general and vague. You either got that shit happenin' or you ain't, baby. He certainly knows, but it's one thing to know and another to pull something through.'

Herbie Hancock 'I don't think he's exactly sure where he wants to steer you, but he kinda throws out something and you work it out with yourself. He might say, "See!" – but you know damn well that wasn't what he was really talking about, not that specific thing. I come up with something and he'll like take the credit for it. But in a way that WAS what he was looking for – for me to stretch.'

Billy Cobham 'Oh man – super-education! He'll come over and he doesn't play drums and he'll sit down and say he wants to show me a figure. OK – here's the sticks, man. And he'll play something and say, "Somethin' like that." Some things he plays I don't even understand how he gets them out, they sound so hip. I can't do them. I think I've learned this from him – to be able to be flexible. If something isn't going your way, then it's just not on the cards, so you go with them. If you can't, then cancel. What Miles does many times is he follows. If he doesn't get exactly what he wants, then he'll just fall in with the flow. When we did *Jack Johnson* Miles didn't have any idea that we were gonna do a shuffle. Just jinga-jinga-jinga-banga. It felt so good that we didn't even have time to get a balance – and Miles said, "Put on the red light!" All the music we'd rehearsed, we never played. Straight feeling!

'Miles has this piano in his house set in behind a crescent couch, into the back of the couch, so he'll say, "See here, man – how's this sound?" Go behind you and play it.'

George Coleman 'Miles had expressed some interest in having me join the band, like around 1959, but I never did. Then he called me in 1963 and told me to cancel my gigs. "You'll be doin' them a favour if you cancel them."

'Miles is a comedian, spontaneous stuff, he comes up with something witty just right off the bat. He'd come up to me and say, "Frank's (Strozier) playin' too long", then he'd go tell Frank, "George is playin' too long." Just his little joke because he'd let you play as long as you wanted.'

Miles Davis 'If you understood everything I said you'd be me.'

CALIFORNIA
COOL

Gerry Mulligan

If California always had the weather, from the forties on it also had its share of leaping residents. Central Avenue, Los Angeles, became the Harlem of the West Coast. With the coming of bebop, as pianist Hampton Hawes wrote in his autobiography, 'the Central Avenue clubs had caught fire and were jumping into the sunrise'. The central figurehead was the native Angelino, six-foot-five tenorman, Dexter Gordon. Before long, Dex was joined in battle on the stand with fellow tenormen Wardell Gray and Teddy Edwards.

'Dexter Gordon was an idol around Central Avenue,' Art Pepper recalled in his autobiography *Straight Life*. 'He was tall. He wore a wide-brimmed hat that made him seem like he was about seven feet tall. He had a stoop to his walk and wore long zoot suits, and he carried his tenor in a sack under his arm. He had these heavy-lidded eyes; he always looked loaded, always had a little half smile on his face. And everybody loved him.'

Pimps, players, hookers, dealers, servicemen and hipsters, black and white – despite LAPD harassment –

flocked to Central Avenue to cop the scene. It was a strutting fashion show: feathers, fob-chains, pinky rings and perfumes, broad satin picture ties and wide-shouldered jackets with rodeo insets and half-belts, slit skirts, long spearpoint collars and longer two-tone co-respondent shoes ('Man, I'm travellin' cow express!'), and black silk stockings rolled to just above the knee.

No wonder out-of-town musicians on Blue Goose buses failed to climb back aboard after the gig. Here's tenorman Brew Moore: 'Billy Faier had a 1949 Buick and somebody wanted him to drive it out to California so he rode through Washington Square shouting "Anyone for the Coast?" And I was just sitting there on a bench and there wasn't shit shaking in New York, so I said "Hell, yes" . . .' a ride that allegedly inspired Kerouac's *On the Road*.

Teddy Edwards was one of the first settlers on Bebop's barbary shore.

Teddy Edwards 'I was touring with the Ernie Fields Orchestra. We played the West Coast and then we went on. The bus broke down above Cheyenne, Wyoming, and all you could see was snow. I thought, you can HAVE all this stuff! I'm going back to California!

'Everybody was in LA because the war was in the Pacific. Soldiers, sailors, whole families had moved to the West. LA was a 24-hour town during that period. I'm sure that the Forties was the most productive period in American history in the arts and everything else. Everything was in full production, employment was at its highest peak, everything was in motion – the military, the machinery for building military equipment, and the money was almost running down the street to meet you!

'Nobody thought about the war hitting America. The whole thing was ALIVE and IN MOTION! America has never been at that tempo before or since. Kids in America now are really doing research on the forties because there are reservoirs of information there that were shelved aside. They're going back, digging it up, finding the clothes, the music, ways to make money and to learn.

'I was fortunate to come through the big bands and the bebop era – a very good time. Central Avenue was a classic street – many clubs like Jack's Basket, Cafe Society, Casablanca, Billy Berg's, Jungle Room. I had great times there with just about everybody. There was a fella around then, he sold records, knew all the solos from all of them. We called him Bebop. He was like the cheer-leader. Sometimes

74

on a blowing session, he'd be pushing me, he'd have everybody going my way, then again he'd be pushing Dexter or Lucky Thompson or Wardell.

'Me and Wardell Gray, we were very close. Lived together, studied together. Two saxophone players: we'd put on a pot of beans, put off our shirts and go to work on those saxophones! He was a fun guy – he played for fun. We played all kinds of jobs together; jobs where we had to split eight dollars a night. I'd go with him on his gig and blow, and he'd come on mine when times were really rough.

'Why did the West Coast go white? I think it was a case of the New York record companies recording mostly black musicians, and the West Coast trying an antidote to that by recording white musicians with the softer sounds. I remember Dick Bock of Pacific Records coming down and saying, "I want everybody but him." Me! That very same guy, me and Wardell, we made the very first record for him that he ever had in his life, and this was how Pacific Records got started.'

Dexter Gordon 'Wearing a hat was part of your thing, you know, on Central Avenue. The cats used to wear hats a lot, and then later the cats started wearing small caps, uh – something like an Eton-type boy's prep school. Standing up to play, that change came with bebop, because obviously it's much easier to play that way when you gotta be more on your toes. But, uh, you still say "sitting in", not "standing in". Hur Hur Hur! Go by somebody's gig, "Hey man – c'n I sit in?"

'Before the war, late thirties, there was very little around LA, so when the big bands came to town it was an occasion. California was isolated from the rest of the country – 3,000 miles from New York, 2,000 from Chicago, 1,500 from Kansas City. It was a jump. But I got a chance to hear Duke, Basie and Lunceford.

'Tenor chases? That was part of the scene then – the jam session thing, the cutting contests. In LA we used to jam all night and every night, but it'd always wind up with me and Wardell. So that's how Ross Russell got the idea of recording us with "The Chase" and "The Steeplechase".

Art Pepper 'At the beginning, when I was very young, playing on Central Avenue and everything, I asked someone about Willie Smith and that he looked so white, and they told me that he was a seventh-grain negro, and I remember wishing that I was. I wanted to be a black because I felt such an affinity to the music.

'Everybody loved Dexter Gordon. All the black cats

and chicks would say, "Heeeeey, Dex!" you know, and pat him on the back and bullshit with him. I used to stand around and marvel at the way they talked. Having really nothing to say, they were able to play these little verbal games back and forth.

'You know that pseudonym I used on Shorty Rogers' *Cool and Crazy* album? Art Salt? I actually had several people ask me, "Have you heard of this guy, Art Salt?" I looked at them because I thought they were just putting me on, real subtle. I said, oh yeah, I've heard of him a little bit. I'm waiting for the joke, you know. "Well," they finally say, "he sure plays a lot like you – but he's black." I can't believe they're serious! See, a long time ago they all thought I was black.'

THE FIFTIES

In the fifties the West Coast polarized along race lines. The music press didn't help, endorsing geographical labels that read: East Coast hot, West Coast cool. The selling white West Coast sound – scored, contrapuntal, infinitely neat, weatherless, often at housebroken decibel levels and all too aware of the European classical heritage – emanated from Miles Davis' *Birth of the Cool* album. Miles' shortlived nine-piece tuba band had an enormous influence. Its melancholy velvet sound and superb arrangements by Gil Evans, Gerry Mulligan, Johnny Carisi and John Lewis, gassed everybody, especially the West Coast cats with a musical schooling, though, commercially, the band could only secure two weeks' work.

The break-up of Stan Kenton's Innovations Orchestra in 1951 left a lot of fine musicians in its wake in the LA area. Most of them found day work in the Hollywood studios, and at night blew for themselves. Record companies like RCA, Capitol, Discovery, Contemporary, Mode and Pacific Jazz were LA based. Howard Rumsey's jazz club, The Lighthouse, at Hermosa Beach, LA's eighty-five seater The Haig and The Blackhawk in San Francisco were the best-known of a swarm of after-hours joints.

Trumpeter Shorty Rogers formed his Giants, most of whom – Bud Shank, Bob Cooper, the Candoli brothers (Pete and Conte), Milt Bernhart, John Graas, Frank Rosolino, Marty Paich and Pete Jolly – became leaders in their own right. In the same year, 1952, Gerry Mulligan formed his trail-blazing piano-less quartet with Chet Baker, and drew national attention following a *Time* magazine story. Art

Pepper and Hampton Hawes formed their band in the same year.

Apart from the characteristic sound of the white West Coast, the movement was sold with a leisure image. Photographer William Claxton's covers for Contemporary albums emphasized primary colours, sunlight, Florida shirts and a general air of relaxation. This West Coast looked like a millionaire's playground. Not for these cats, said the cover art, the smoke and shadows of the East Coast jazz cellars. The musicians were photographed playing golf, getting out of rowing boats in wet-suits, lounging against trees and discovering driftwood. *Music For Lighthouse Keeping*, an album featuring the ex-Kentonites of Howard Rumsey's All Stars, typically shows the leader propped against a bright red hydrant under a blithe blue sky with palm trees and the lighthouse in back. Even Sonny Rollins, an East Coast visitor, was photographed as a gunslinger next to the skull of a steer and a cactus.

Throughout the fifties, LA's great black musicians like Dexter Gordon, Harold Land, Sonny Criss and Teddy Edwards had a thin time of it.

Shelly Manne 'I used to enjoy working in the studios, not because it was an outlet for jazz, but it was creative at one time. I made a lotta money, but it used to be more fun. I couldn't just settle for studio. Whenever jazz jobs came, studio work was secondary. I never went away from jazz, and when I had my club, Shelly's Mannehole, I was playing three or four times a week.'

Shorty Rogers 'A lot of people talk about a West Coast *sound* – discuss all kinds of influences like Miles Davis' tuba band and how, for some tastes, it wasn't exciting enough. Well, I believe you're a product of your heritage. Shelly Manne and I went back forty-two years . . . we grew up with the Basie Band and the Kansas City Seven: 'Sweets' Edison playing mute, Pres doubling on clarinet. And, with The Giants, all that Jimmy Giuffre, Shelly and myself were attempting was to update that flavour.'

Gerry Mulligan 'My music did have a sombre sound to it in context with other music, and it took me a long time to evolve out of it. That's where I was with the early quartet, and Chet Baker too had a very mournful sound. In a musical way, Chet and I had an uncanny relationship in that first quartet – more so since I didn't really like to be around him and he didn't like to be around me. That's what made the musical relationship more incredible. Personally, we were so un-

Top: *Wardell and Dexter*
Below: *Wardell Grey, Stan Getz and Zoot Sims*
Right: *Shelly Manne*

suited to each other.

'The basic idea of that quartet was that we should all play on an acoustical level where the bass could function naturally. The bass was an important line in that group. You had to hear it. It opened up the possibility of a kind of contrapuntal playing that is not possible when you play louder.

'Chet and I found it so easy to play together. We were always able to anticipate what the other one was going to do. Some nights with that quartet, we'd play without ever discussing what we were going to play. One or the other would just start playing and the other would pick it up, and the audience would never know the difference. When we'd done with it, it sounded like an intricately worked out arrangement. We'd make endings that'd make my hair stand on end!'

MR CHET

A MODERN DAY TRAGEDY

They still haunt the dressing-room – the gutter press and the older women – the notion probably being to dust off the good old '3,000 Hell-Holes In My Arm' feature, and save him from himself, respectively. The Chet Baker story is the stuff of movies all right, and back in 1962 Dino de Laurentiis toyed with the project as a role for Robert Wagner, until the Italian narcotics squad cornered the subject for a seventeen-month stretch.

None of this interests Chet Baker in the least. Music is the core of his life, the search for tonal beauty and spontaneous symmetry, and jazz biopics never do much on that. He has always been sold along extra-musical lines, and has learned to live with it. There was always a sucking gap between the image and the man – the demands of the press, the polls and the bobbysoxers threatening to drain off his oxygen.

In a way, we've all seen The Chet Baker Story anyway.

In 1950, when *Young Man With A Horn* was packing them in to see Kirk Douglas handle a trumpet, the young Chesney H. Baker was re-enlisting in a San Francisco-based Army band so that he could sit in at the city's night-spots and jam. In 1953, when doomed and handsome Montgomery Clift was playing taps for a dead buddy in *From Here To Eternity*, Chet was winding up the association with Gerry Mulligan which had rocketed him to stardom, and in 1956, when *The Man With The Golden Arm* hit the screens, Chet got himself a habit.

Success, as Art Blakey says, can be a pie in the face. In 1953, *Downbeat*'s twenty-four-year-old New Star was being smothered with praise by his fans for his pretty sound and his pretty face. He was the boy-next-door, the sound of introspection on a summer evening fire-escape, the sorority successor to Bix.

'I suppose I was conscious of that in a way', says Chet in

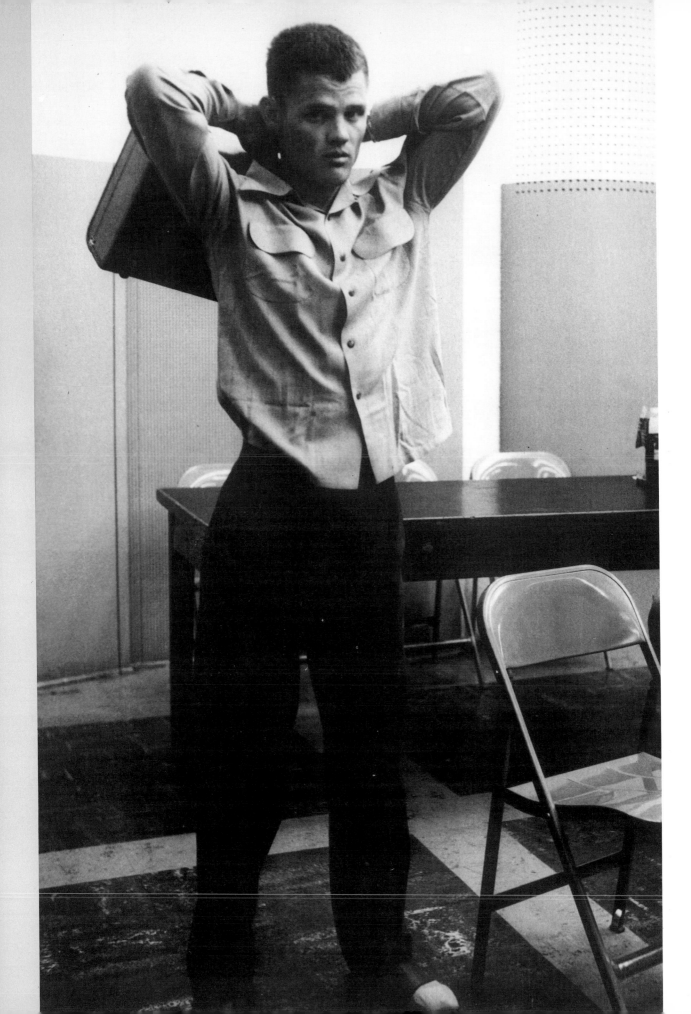

his faint Oklahoma country-boy voice. 'I was never really content with the sound and I kept trying to develop, looking for what I had in the back of my mind. Being able to play with or without vibrato, and being able to play, intonation-wise, right in the centre. It's just trying to get out the end of the horn something that has a quality and a uniqueness that doesn't sound like somebody else. You know, it seems the people are only impressed by three things – either you play fast, or you play high, or by the sound of the instrument itself. It's not what notes you play.' He shrugs tiredly.

Chet's rise to stardom was one of those overnight affairs that you pay for later. Charlie Parker picked him to share the front line during his stay on the West Coast, and they toured together through California, Oregon and Canada. 'Bird treated me sorta like a son. He wouldn't let anybody approach me with anything, any kinda drugs – and they tried to. He would really get upset. He himself was drinking a coupla fifths of Hennessey cognac at that time, and snorting stuff. He had no car, and I would drive him around . . .'

He joined Gerry Mulligan's piano-less quartet in 1952, and stayed nine months. It was long enough to grab the attention of the jazz hipsters. His melancholy tone and simple lyricism seemed to linger in the nerve endings long after the last notes had sounded. It was a restricted style, based on the cool Miles Davis, and it offered a marginal, windscreen-wiper view of the possibilities of jazz trumpet – but it cast a magical spell. He laid the definitive 'My Funny Valentine'.

Chet's *Downbeat* award was announced while Mulligan was serving time for narcotics. When Gerry hit the street again, Chet's asking price had gone up. He'd formed his own quartet with pianist Russ Freeman, and wasn't interested in returning to the old band for 125 bucks a week. They parted on bad terms, and Chet went on to earn over two grand a week. Everything was going right for him – even his singing career, a second-string to his bow in case a gum disorder put the trumpet out of action. And his voice cast the same forlorn, little-boy-lost shadow, causing co-eds to swoon clean out of their saddle Oxfords. He was James Dean, Sinatra and Bix, rolled into one.

In 1956, disaster struck. Chet got hooked. By 1959, he'd had seven drugs busts, lost his New York cabaret card, and served time on Rikers Island and Lucca Prison, Italy. In 1962 Germany deported him, and in 1963 Britain jailed him, then deported him. After an argument with his connection in San Francisco, five guys stomped him, splintering his

teeth and busting his lip. The skull started to show through the boy-next-door looks. He became notorious, detained for hours on the frontiers of Europe while customs rummaged his luggage and his person, haunted by gossip columnists looking for easy jazz-and-junk copy. It became difficult to get bookings.

Chet's obsession with music remained intact, but the image altered. Now he was sold as the doomed Flying Dutchman of jazz. In Naples, they stole his trumpet right off the piano, hoping the sound came along with the horn. The critics, embarrassed by having over-praised him at the start, now lowered the boom. His playing was insipid, lifeless, they said, and his singing was a joke. Whatever, the musician played on, glueing his dentures against his palate to take the strain of the instrument.

And the loyal would catch glimpses of him, always travelling, usually alone. On a wet night in a tank town in the Midlands, Chet stands gazing in the window of a pawnshop. In among the unredeemed typewriters, chromeband wrist-watches and radios, is a silver trumpet in a battered blue case. Hatless, the camel overcoat missing its belt, Chet stands in the rain contemplating the trumpet. He's close enough to cloud the glass. It could be a movie, the wet surfaces tremulous enough to dissolve back into some Oklahoma childhood footage of yearning in knee-pants.

'What was I doing? Oh, I was trying to see the name. You never know what a horn like that is gonna sound like.'

Snapshots of the wanderer. In Stryker's Bar, New York City, Lee Konitz and Wilbur Little have pulled a house of about twelve cats for their duet. Nobody bothered to open the back of the bar where the tables are. Suddenly, a third instrument nudges shyly into the unravelling lines. Konitz's eyes blinked open and closed again. He knew who it was from the sound, long before the light caught the trumpet player with the big African amethyst ring on his little finger. Nobody had seen him come in, and he was sitting there in gloom, feet on a chair, head bowed, playing. 'Hey, baby,' murmured the bartender, almost under his breath. 'It's Mister Chet.'

His comeback started in the early seventies with the Methadone programme, and Dizzy Gillespie – one of the kindest cats in the business – got him a booking at New York's Half Note. Since then, Chet has been twice as punctual as anyone else, and turned inward to avoid the whisperers and the pointing fingers and the knowing nudges. A new generation fell under Chet's spell. Elvis Costello, who had paid tribute to the trumpeter on his own 'My Funny

CHET BAKER IN EUROPE
A JAZZ TOUR OF THE NATO COUNTRIES

PACIFIC JAZZ 1218

Ciao Chet

Valentine' and 'Almost Blue', hired him to solo on his version of 'Shipbuilding'. The French film director, Bertrand Tavernier, signed him up for a song in *Round Midnight*, the jazz movie. Tricks are walking again.

'I play every set as though it was my last,' he says, without melodramatics. 'I want to show the musicians I'm playing with that I'm still giving it all I've got. We're just up there to play music. And that's all.'

More than enough, Mister Chet.

81

THE ART
OF DRUMS

'Through this portal pass prospects for the world's finest fighting force' – a claim just as befitting to the Jazz Messengers as those young volunteers confronted by this legend over the gates of the US Marines' Training Camp at Parris Island, South Carolina.

For thirty years and more, Art Blakey's band has been both boot camp and actor's studio for those musicians prepared to push themselves beyond the limit or burn-out in the process. In doing so, the Messengers have shaped the style of most small group blowin' for three decades.
Two events in 1955: the passing of Bird and the continued cool breeze from California, motivated the Big Apple to again reinforce its once undisputed reputation as Jazz City USA.

Five years of commercially successful cool had shut off large sections of black music. But, as West Coast jazz became too clever for its own survival – gimmicky instrumentation and over-arrangement – the East Coast flexed a collective muscle and retaliated with Hard Bop. By July 1955, Miles had been 'rediscovered' at Newport (and would soon team with 'Trane); Monk had come in out of the cold to sign with Riverside; Dizzy again fronted a Big Band; Max Roach–Clifford Brown Inc. (with Sonny Rollins) were almost as big a draw as the MJQ and Jay & Kai; Cannonball Adderley and Donald Byrd were the year's New Stars, Jimmy Smith was about to launch himself as the Next Big Thing and Art Blakey's Jazz Messengers had just taped their wondrous Blue Note début at Café Bohemia.

The two horn plus three rhythm format common to Hard Bop may have adhered to Bird's bop blueprint, but the approach had now become more formally organized.

Drums moved up to the front line, pianists were equally percussive, making catapults for soloists, and the simplification of melodies made the new style into a fist.

Hitting a groove became essential.

Though synonymous with New York City, this new brand of hard blown bop wasn't restricted to just one locale. Back on the coast, Art Pepper and Jack Sheldon displayed just as much chutzpah – the former recording one of his best-ever albums with the Miles Davis rhythm section.

The new music was ripe for drastically improved recording techniques (as pioneered by Rudy Van Gelder) and the mass acceptance of the 12-inch LP. No longer did bop sound like a wasp under a tumbler. This hard edge was further derived from the new breed who, like Clifford Brown, Johnny Griffin, Hank Mobley and Art Farmer had served time with either Hampton or in chittlin' circuit R&B combos.

Hitting harder seemed second nature as the music often ran as a parallel soundtrack to the emergence of the NAACP and Black Consciousness.

Soul Brother Ray Charles was a big influence on Hard Bop. The small instrumental combo that waxed *The Great Ray Charles* caught the ear of both Art Blakey and Horace Silver, dictating the Messengers' funky feel – the sanctified side being exemplified by 'The Preacher' which came complete with gospel figures and a Baptist back-beat. The Jazz Messengers proper lasted from February 1955 until June of the following year when a split between Blakey and Silver prompted the pianist to decamp with Donald Byrd (who'd replaced Kenny Dorham), Hank Mobley and Doug Watkins, leaving the drummer with the corporate name and any remaining goodwill.

Like any sharp leader, Blakey insists his current

AND HIS GRETSCH DRUMS.

line-up to be his best yet, but will admit special affection for the 'Café Bohemia' band. 'Kenny Dorham (phew)... he was somethin'... Hank Mobley too. Great musicians both.' The grooming of the prodigious Marsalis brothers – Wynton and Branford – as all-purpose role models for both a new generation of jazz players and listeners has thrown the spotlight back on to Blakey's College of Knowledge and its astonishing history of excellence – particularly in the trumpet department, which commenced with Clifford Brown by way of Kenny Dorham, Donald Byrd, Bill Hardman, Lee Morgan, Freddie Hubbard, Chuck Mangione, Woody Shaw, Randy Brecker and, Wynton's equally accomplished replacement, Terence Blanchard. Elsewhere, Blakey's hard fast boppers include super-saxists Jackie McLean, Hank Mobley, Johnny Griffin, Benny Golson, Wayne Shorter, Bobby Watson, trombonists Curtis Fuller and Slide Hampton and a parade of two-fisted pianists from Horace Silver through Bobby Timmons, Junior Mance, Cedar Walton, McCoy Tyner, Chick Corea, George Cables, Keith Jarrett, JoAnne Brackeen and Walter Davis Jr.

Not only did the majority graduate to Blue Note's artists' roster, but the likes of Timmons and Shorter carved successful careers both as solo stars and with Cannonball Adderley's Quintet and Weather Report. Said hit composer Bobby Timmons, 'Art Blakey is a leader who builds other leaders.'

Art Blakey gives the appearance of having been carved out of a solid block of black granite. Stocky and square-jawed, his bulging muscles are bound with taut steel cable veins. He could beat drums for ever.

'Jazz drums wouldn't be the same if it weren't for Art Blakey,' insists that equally percussive pianist Cecil Taylor.

Indeed, this new form of super-dynamic power-drumming as pioneered by Art Blakey, Max Roach and Philly Joe Jones caused critical outcry on account of noise levels and the drummers' dominance.

Art Blakey is an unrelenting player – directing activity from his drum stool, prodding and punctuating the front-line horn player's train of improvisation. His signature is unmistakeable: the double-tempo sprints, press rolls of China Syndrome meltdown ferocity, crushing high-hat chops, rattling rim shots – an avalanche of skin and Zildjian which can momentarily swamp the entire band before the shock waves roll back and everyone surfaces for air.

From his early days with 'Mr B's' big band to Birdland be-bopping with Bird, Dizzy and Monk, the name of Art Blakey has always been synonymous with innovation.

Do the rookies give him a hard run?
'Are you kiddin'!! None of them have nearly as much vitality as me. Listen to the records... hear for yourself... I'm always kickin' 'em in the ass. It's as much as they can do to keep up with me. When they join they're scared to death ... most of 'em grow up and die! When they join the Messengers, the bullshit's over. On the bandstand, I demand *not* 99 per cent, I want 110 per cent and nothing less. See, you can't play down to the people, 'cause they paid their money to get in.'

And the vanity of stars?
'*They're* just a bunch of damn fools – people don't need 'em. They're just lucky enough to be paid for doin' somethin' they like to do. You're not on stage to be worshipped – it's just another job.'

Following the break-up of the original Dorham/Mobley/ Silver/Watkins line-up, it took a period of internal adjustment before the Messengers once again reasserted themselves and returned to Blue Note. Just how big a setback it can be when key sidemen leave, Blakey reveals: 'Let's get one thing straight – they don't quit... I fire 'em. When they get too big, I can't afford to pay them – it's time for them to leave. There's always other kids waiting in line just like any employment agency. I'm not running a post office – this is the Jazz Messengers! When they leave, I wish them well, but I'm not about to worry about who I'm gonna replace them with.

'I haven't got the time to go looking for musicians – *they* find *me*. My reputation precedes me. Young musicians who feel they've got what it takes to become a Messenger know who I am and how to find me – only then do we see if they're as hot as they think they are! Anyway, when someone leaves the Messengers they're obliged to nominate their successor. Now, it's just as important to their own reputation to see that the vacant position is filled by the best available player. That's how we got Terence Blanchard. When it was time for Wynton Marsalis to become a leader, that's who he nominated as his replacement.'
But there have been occasions when the departure of key sidemen has appeared almost catastrophic?
'When I could no longer afford to keep Lee Morgan, Benny Golson and Bobby Timmons, I brought in Freddie Hubbard, Wayne Shorter, Curtis Fuller and Cedar Walton – good musicians, but a lotta people thought, "There goes the Jazz Messengers."

'They reckoned the new band was full of musicians who couldn't play! Wayne Shorter!! They'd say he sounds like he's scrambling eggs!! Anyway, once when we were all taking a breather outside Birdland, Coltrane sneaked up behind us and whispered, "Hey, but it's the way Wayne Shorter scrambles those eggs!"

'You gotta understand, any line-up I get is successful . . . it's gonna sound like the Jazz Messengers and why? Because *I* am there . . . I am *the* Messenger; I'm the one directing traffic. All my bands sound like the Jazz Messengers because Art Blakey is there. If Art Blakey is not there, then they'll sound like somethin' else altogether. It's my style . . . I'm the leader. So it doesn't make no difference who comes or goes, I can always handle it.

'Nobody comes in as a star . . . I don't need no stars . . . no prima donnas. I make the group the star. I'm not the star, the whole group is the star.'

The Jazz Messengers have been fortunate enough to attract players sufficiently skilled as writers to contribute to the band's already impressive pad. What if a player can't cut it as a composer? 'Simple, they gotta learn real fast if they're ever gonna join the Messengers. Like, when Horace Silver was first in the band, he was constantly moanin', "I *can't* write." "You better write," I said, "or you're fired!" Now, he'll tell you, "Thank God for Art Blakey, he *made* me write." All those hits . . . they take care of him . . . made him rich.

'Horace wasn't the only one. Some great writers came through the band – Hank Mobley, Benny Golson, Bobby Timmons . . . I particularly like Wayne Shorter's music. The music he wrote for the Messengers is still amongst his best. Currently, I've got Terence Blanchard.'

So what, these past thirty years, has Blakey offered his sidemen that no other bandleader can?

'I can swing my ass off – that's what!' he chortles. 'I ain't heard no other drummer play "Blues March" – it's nuthin' but *swing*. Trouble nowadays, they don't teach young drummers the most important thing of all – how to swing . . . just teach 'em how to play the dish towel. Drums should get to the soul. It's the second instrument. First, there's the human voice and then there's the drum.

'If you can't identify yourself on a record, you're in trouble. No good sounding like Buddy Rich, Gene Krupa or Dave Tough – *they* made their mark. A drummer can't feel what they feel. Sure, he may play the same licks, but that's not the same thing.

'Same goes for electric drums – pull the plug and you've

got nuthin' . . . can't play no more than the electronics allow, so what's that all about! They're just gadgets and only Herbie Hancock and Miles Davis have done anything remotely worthwhile in that area. Me! I don't wanna know – ain't interested.

'Everyone can't be Thelonious Monk and I'm Art Blakey and I'm proud of what I've done, because I believe in what I do. Sure, I like disco – like to go and dance, but play it? No!'

Any conversation with Art Blakey invariably touches upon Monk's all-embracing legacy. Acknowledged as the one drummer to ever fully accommodate the pianist, Blakey maintains that not only is it an honour for him to be mentioned in the same breath, but that Monk's repertoire remains the ultimate test of a player's true worth.

'Today, musicians in my band are on top of Monk's music, but at the time Monk wrote it, musicians were scared to play his material – said it was much too hard.

'Nowadays, they tell you Stevie Wonder is a genius because he makes all those cash tills ring, but I ain't never seen an armoured security van following a hearse. The only thing that follows you is respect. That's why I stay active, why I stay healthy and, that's why I'm still fighting hard. See, the pendulum swung the other way – young people haven't been given a choice . . . jazz has been hidden from them. Only now they're beginning to discover it for themselves.

'They've never seen Charlie Parker . . . never seen John Coltrane . . . never seen Lee Morgan and the first time they hear musicians of that calibre, it's a real shock. Makes 'em question the worth of most of the stuff they've been fed over the radio.

'People should like all music, but it does seem that for far too many years jazz was treated like some big military secret. That's tragic because the highest level of performance on any musical instrument comes through jazz – it's spiritual.'

THE MAN WITH THE GOLDEN ARM

A FILM BY OTTO PREMINGER

JAZZ IN THE MOVIES

SCORING FOR THE STUDIOS

INTRODUCTION

The USA has surfaced two great art forms this century, and proved itself incapable of combining them. Jazz and film share many characteristics, but, as far as back home is concerned, no possibilities of creative union. Colour used to be the stumbling block; crassness still is. Billie Holiday was relegated to lady's maid to a star nobody can now remember in *New Orleans*, and, nearly forty years on, Richard Gere had to be drafted in to give *Cotton Club* Caucasian credibility.

If black jazz is still becalmed among the hoofing Pullman porters and happy darkie gatherings of Hollywood, white jazz has at least suffered the same screen fate as Liszt and Tchaikovsky. Hollywood can handle the all-purpose misunderstood white genius – the garret, the bottle, the rumpled wig over trumpet, manuscript paper or canvas, and the girl across the landing who understands. Most jazz vehicles have hit on the legend of Bix Beiderbecke: live fast, die young, and have a good-looking corpse for the New Orleans funeral.

Usually, jazz is peripheral to the story, even when the star is cast as a jazz musician. Steve McQueen could have been a plumber for all the difference it made to *Love With The Proper Stranger*. Even boxing has done better, with *The Set Up* and *Raging Bull* probing into the professional motivations of the protagonists. Of all American jazz feature films, only *Pete Kelly's Blues* and *New York, New York* have caught the milieu on the hoof, avoiding the pitfalls of the jazz biopic, that sense that the scriptwriters worked out of some lexicon of hip jargon.

For Hollywood, jazz is what blares up on the soundtrack when the star goes to the bad. The solitary saxophone spells night loneliness. Screen hookers rate jazz too, mashing potatoes in the lap as they slink through the cigarette smoke of some jazz joint. Glossy pieces of swingin' nothing for Anthony Franciosa, and Ann Margret used West Coast or Bossa Nova to grease the groove.

Nevertheless, Hollywood movies *were* made which – ignorant of the value of the cats sent by Central Casting – have become jazz collectors' items. Illinois Jacquet scored a chorus in *DOA*, and Shorty Rogers and Shelly Manne a few lines in *The Man With The Golden Arm*. Back in 1941, Orson Welles planned on making a jazz movie epic, but the project remained on the shelf. Maybe one day, one of the jazz-fan film directors – Mel Brooks, Clint Eastwood, Woody Allen – will get it on, but meanwhile the hip moviegoers look to Europe. So far, the Swedish *Sven Klang's Combo* and the French *Round Midnight* have come closest to a dignified marriage of sight and cooking sounds.

Left: *Robert Wagner (*All The Fine Young Cannibals*)*
Right: *Tony Curtis and Red Norvo (*The Kings Go Forth*)*
Above: *Kirk Douglas and Hoagy Carmichael (*Young Man With A Horn*)*

LALO SCHIFRIN

Most jazzmen who have composed for the movies have retired hurt. Too many cooks cutting up the quavers. Duke Ellington scored *Anatomy of a Murder* for Otto Preminger, but little else of significance. Gil Evans has done *Absolute Beginners*, and Mingus *Shadows*. There's an old Hollywood writers' quote that also applies to the experience of jazz composers in Tinseltown. 'They ruin your stories. They massacre your ideas. They prostitute your art. They trample on your pride. And what do you get for it? A fortune.'

A handful have made the crossover. Shorty Rogers, Jay Jay Johnson, Oliver Nelson, Quincy Jones and Herbie Hancock seem able to knock a note on the celluloid, reap the fortune, and step back on to the jazz scene without loss of artistic credibility. The champ has to be Argentinian pianist-composer, Lalo Schifrin. He's scored over seventy movies, including *Dirty Harry*, *Bullitt*, *Magnum Force*, *Cool Hand Luke*, *The Cincinnati Kid*, *The Four Musketeers* and *Murderers' Row*, and more TV, like 'Starsky & Hutch' and 'Mission Impossible', than you'd want to remember. And when he has time, he sits in on the stand with his bebop buddies.

'I was three years on the road with Dizzy Gillespie. That's a long time. I was looking for a sedentary place to write, and Hollywood was the best place from every point of view. It allowed me to write whatever I wanted and also experiment. I always liked film, and I'd already done some film scores in South America.

'Film making is not an individual art form. It's a collective, almost like a jazz jam session. For instance, the bass player has his own jurisdiction, providing the backbone of the rhythm. The drummer is completing that with the pianist – the harmonic-rhythmic backbone. You can apply the same thing to films. It's a gestalt. The director is the brain; the cameraman is the eyes; the film editor is the DNA; the producer is the lungs; and the composer is the ears.

89

'To write a film score, you have to have a special sensitivity for audio-visual counterpoint. Many musicians attempt to write for films, but they don't have a sense of the dramatic, or a sense of the texture of the film against the texture of the music. Even very good musicians fail, and mainly it was because they were taking over, they were over-scoring. The idea is to combine. Sometimes a lack of music can be very good. It is unnecessary to duplicate what is in the film, because to duplicate is just parallel motion.'

Schifrin has found his own Dizzy Gillespies in Hollywood among his craft – film composers who know that their contribution can shorten a scene, motivate the most neutral activity, and carry thematic reminders on a subtler level than vision. 'The real reason for music', said Bernard Herrmann, who scored *Citizen Kane*, *The Magnificent Ambersons*, *Psycho*, *The Birds* and *Taxi Driver*, 'is that a piece of film, by its nature, lacks a certain ability to convey emotional overtones.' Like Schifrin, Herrmann had an abhorrence of the pop jingle concession that sells in the foyer along with the T-shirt of the movie. 'All pop songs are based on an eight-bar phrase, so once they start the melody, they've got to finish it. It has to last that long. It goes along with the picture: it doesn't go with it.'

Where screen writers complain about being cut, film composers, in Lalo Schifrin's experience, suffer the reverse. Themes written for specific characters get spread over the whole cast like catsup. He has done everything from hack work to labours of love, and takes the long view.

'I did the insect film, *The Hellstrom Chronicle*, which won a prize at Cannes. I did everything. There was no boundary between sound effects and music. I used avant-garde techniques combining electronics and fifty string players using wire brushes instead of bows for the battle of the ants. These are the kind of things that push your imagination to the limit. But even television can be creative. For example, in *Medical Center* they have a main title where an ambulance is coming from the distance. I took a Moog synthesizer and imitated the siren, kept it going up and up and when it reached a pitch – it became the melody. These are little things you can have fun with.

'There isn't so much fun in jazz today. There are too many monks about – and there is only one MONK, huh. The beboppers didn't talk all that mysticism.'

Straightman interviewer: 'What did they talk about?'

Lalo Schifrin: 'Who gives good head.'

Eddie 'Lockjaw' Davis 'In films they had jazz whenever two thugs were plotting a bank raid. The nice scene between the hero and the heroine had violins, violas. It's always been associated in the public mind with the delinquent son or the runaway daughter or thieves.'

Laurie Pepper 'Jerry Fielding called Art up for *The*

Enforcer and asked him if he played baritone. Art said, "Uh...uh...yeah." Art had played baritone in prison one time because that was the only available horn. So Jerry said great, because Gerry Mulligan wanted too much money. Art went in, and there were all these studio guys who are ex-Kentonites, all old jazz players all sitting round the studio – and Art walks in with his baritone. Everybody BUT Jerry Fielding knew Art Pepper was NOT a baritone player!'

Art Pepper 'He asked someone if I could read music too.'

Benny Golson '*Des Femmes Disparaissent*? I wrote all that music in the studio. The Jazz Messengers had to stay all night round the clock until next morning. They'd show me a cue and tell me how many minutes it was, and I'd write a piece of music. The other guys'd lollygag and talk, and when I'd got it done, they'd come back and record it.

'*Where It's At*? That one I want you to forget. Now I'm embarrassed. I don't think anyone ever found out where it was at, including me. I had a thirst for movie work when I first went out to Hollywood from New York in 1967, but a coupla years ago my thirst was satisfied. It's such a rat race trying to second guess the producers.'

Shorty Rogers 'For a long time, The Lighthouse was the focal point for jazz in LA, the West Coast equivalent of Birdland, except that a lot of movie people were always dropping by. Composer Leith Stevens was a regular and through him I got to work on *The Wild One*.

'Brando had control over the soundtrack and he asked Stevens for suggestions. Stevens gave him some current LPs including my *Modern Sounds* ten-inch for Capitol. "I want *that* guy," Brando told Stevens after he'd heard the album. So Stevens composed the themes and I arranged them in exactly the same way I would have done for either Stan Kenton's Orchestra or my own Giants.

'I had the same composer/arranger partnership with Elmer Bernstein on *The Man With The Golden Arm*. I also got to play a scene with Sinatra. Trouble was, I kept blowing my lines. Otto Preminger, who was directing, was demonic. "Get rid of *that* kid," meaning me, he shouted so everyone can hear. "I want a real actor!" Sinatra wouldn't hear of it. "Shorty stays," Sinatra told Preminger. And I spent the entire lunchbreak with Sinatra rehearsing the scene, so that when shooting restarted, we did it in one take. It was the end of my acting career.'

Shelly Manne 'Was I on *The Last Detail*? I can't remember. Probably was. I was doing two or three a week, and I didn't always see the title. Often it hadn't got one. On the music it says M25062. There are no more jazz scores. They might have me playing the hi-hat – ha-da-da, ha-da-da – but that doesn't mean it's a jazz score. Closest to a jazz score was *I Want To Live* that Johnny Mandel wrote, or the way we useta do *Peter Gunn* with Hank Mancini. He'd use jazz musicians for what they could do, and sometimes we'd just look at a scene and improvise. A line would come across the screen to tell you when to start, and a line to tell you when it should end.

'*The Man With The Golden Arm* wasn't jazz. It was jazz-oriented music. I helped Sinatra with the look of playing drums, how to hold the brushes, little things, but he'd been in big bands, watched drummers all his life. I played Dave Tough in *The Five Pennies* and *The Gene Krupa Story*. Davey'd been a close friend. I'd had to go out and identify his body in the funeral home. We useta hang out together.

'Hollywood has never made a good film about jazz. I don't know why. Those films aren't real. Most of the time you read the script and it's the director's or producer's viewpoint, and outsiders don't understand. Hollywood always has the bus driving down the road with the band jamming in the back. They call it a jazz picture, but the jazz is always in the background, and it ends up being the same love story, boy loves girl. But those bus scenes in *New York, New York* were real. That came close to capturing the feeling of the big bands on the road at that time. *The Gene Krupa Story* just skimmed along the surface.'

Buddy de Franco 'I remember the Tommy Dorsey band doing *Thrill Of Romance* in the forties. Big picture. Lotta money. Van Heflin and Esther Williams. The producer wanted an authentic jazz jam session. He told us, "You know, where you guys have been playing for dancing and you go somewhere and you sit in? That's what we want." So Tommy said fine, we could provide that, and organized a little jazz session with Buddy Rich, Dodo Marmarosa, Ziggy Elman and me.

'So we got to the studio and we play. The producer said to Dodo, "Do you always hunch over the piano when you play?" We explained that Dodo was deformed, the big head and everything. Then the producer said to me, "Why do you play the clarinet down? Put the clarinet up in the air." He pointed at the ceiling and they marked it with chalk. "Hit that. Fix your eyes on that light." We played some more. Then he said, "It's not working out right. Let's get some French-Canadian soldiers to come in and they'll sing 'Alouette', and you'll jazz up 'Alouette'." With that, Tommy Dorsey hit the ceiling.'

Bertrand Tavernier (directed *Round Midnight*, starring Dexter Gordon) 'I'd always been worried by actors when they were playing jazzmen, whether it was Paul Newman in *Paris Blues* or even the best performance which I've seen, which was Robert De Niro in *New York, New York*. Even that had some flaws. When De Niro played, it was technically perfect – but I could see he was not *listening*.

'As soon as I started to think about this project, *Round Midnight*, I decided it would be much more interesting to try a musician as an actor, rather than the reverse. There were precise gestures, movements, some relationship between the musician and the reed that I'd seen in documentaries, but that I'd never found in any feature film – except *Sven Klang's Combo*, and they were really playing. I saw a film of Dexter Gordon in concert that I found absolutely stunning! The way he was moving his hands, the way he was walking, the movement of his feet – everything! Dexter was unique.

'You have to be a little bit angry when you make a film, I think, and I made *Round Midnight* as a reaction against the way black musicians have always been treated by Hollywood, and by their country. I've been so offended by the way Hollywood has treated jazz. When you think that people like Charlie Parker, Mingus and Monk were hardly used for film scores. I mean, when they were doing *Young Man With A Horn* it was Harry James playing trumpet for Kirk Douglas, which is not bad, but...

'*Cotton Club*? I see no reason for anybody to do *Cotton Club*. Nobody studied the music carefully in terms of the way it was *felt* at that time. I don't see any scene which tells me why the film was made.'

Dexter Gordon 'I was in *Unchained*. I was in Chino Penitentiary when they were filming. Hal Bartlett movie, starred Crazylegs Hirsch. They used me for a jam session scene. When the movie came out, somebody else had dubbed my tenor solo.'

Robert Altman 'I am a jazz fan. Shelly Manne was a great friend of mine. I met him when I was making *The James Dean Story*. Did you know I was originally going to do *Cotton Club*? I was just thrilled by the idea – I mean, for twelve years that club was a whole social history. Well, finally I said to the producer, Bob Evans, you take it and make it, and he gave it to Francis Coppola. Richard Gere as a trumpet player? No, not at all! It doesn't make any sense. Why fuck up the jazz? *Jazz On A Summer's Day* – that's as good as you'll get.'

92

Top: *Dexter Gordon* ('Round Midnight)
Below: *Frank Sinatra and Shorty Rogers*
(The Man with the Golden Arm)
Right: *Jack Webb* (Pete Kelly's Blues)

THE METHOD
MAKES
THE SCENE

*Karl Malden and Marlon Brando (*A Streetcar Named Desire*)*

For the teenage moviegoer on the cusp of the fifties, Marlon hit the chord that rocked the spinet. It was a generation that hadn't known what to do with its hands, who to be, what to wear, and, more importantly, how to secede from a society in which even emcees at hops came on like aldermen laying a marble stone. In the postwar years, history may have worn a rose, but the kids – waiting for someone to throw a six to start – were unfailingly underfoot. For them, sociologically speaking, shit wasn't shakin'.

The Method circled the block for a moment before walloping into focus. The first punk of spring was Montgomery Clift, standing on a dusty mid-Western highway thumbing a lift. He wore a white T-shirt, a leather Second World War bomber jacket, fat pants, and he carried a cheap fibre suitcase. With an odd choreography of self-absorbed gestures, he swung up into the cab of a truck. The date is 1951, and Clift is sketching a visual prototype in the pre-credit sequence for *A Place In The Sun*. For that moment, Clift could be Kerouac. Method and Hipster were coming together.

The previous year had seen the debut of Marlon Brando in *The Men*, but since he was playing a paraplegic with a grudge against legs, few identified. Then came *A Streetcar Named Desire*. Cast as the brutal, crafty Polack, Stanley Kowalski, Brando had nothing for the kids to identify with, except for the image. Wearing his torn T-shirt like a flag, biceps, identity chain, chuggalugging the Schlitz, chucking the radio out of the window – 'Cut the rebop!' – Stanley was one in the eye for Joe College. He was the body vivid and the instinct enthroned.

'I detest the character', said Brando, and fled the scene for Mexico (*Viva Zapata!*) and Ancient Rome (*Julius Caesar*). But Hip was the magnet that glued him to the plate, and the next thing the teenager in the stalls saw was Johnnie, the mixed-up motorcycle kid, brooming into sleepy Squaresville, bearing his trophies like burial urns on his handlebars in *The Wild One*, but no grace, no ambiguity.

The film was terrible. Made in 1954, it wasn't released in Britain until 1968, by which time that sedition was stagnant with oversubscribed Chapters and leather gays. 'We started out to do something worthwhile, to explain the

psychology of the hipster. But somewhere along the way we went off the track. The Breen Office forbade any dialogue about motorcycles, gangs and kicks as a release from the sheer bum-numbing dullness of day-jobs, but – DAMN! – the project was self-defeating from the whistle! You don't explain the hipster. Which is why the only couplet anybody ever remembers from the movie counters a question with a question: Sheriff – 'What are you rebelling against, kid?' Johnnie – 'Watcha got?'

On The Waterfront looked like the last of Brando's one-way tickets to Palookaville: the grace and power of the body in its lumpy Iron Boy work-clothes, the eloquence of gesture against the stumbling inadequacy of speech. Against the grey background of Hoboken's docks, Brando's Terry Malloy sits on a playground swing trying to fit his boxer's mitt into a girl's glove. Dim, punchy, inarticulate, he tries to chat her up. 'I don't like the country. The crickets keep me awake.' But his hand sings a tender message, almost listening to the strains and fits of the glove.

Brando ran again. 'It made me look like an asshole. I was the hot copy boy who scratched his ass and pissed on the rug.' Hipsters had to wait – and sit through scores of

impersonations – until Brando came back to base with *Last Tango In Paris*, 1972. We had been tantalized with bulletins about the star hanging out with bebop tenorman Allen Eager, belting bongos after hours. Now he came all the way out of the basket on Henry Miller/Charles Bukowski turf as the ageing Paul, screwing, screaming, shaking the bars, rapping non-stop like Neal Cassady or dumb with incommunicable connections. It was the rhythm of the hipster and, to underline the affinities, here was tenorman Gato Barbieri ripping through the soundtrack.

Back in the fifties the new young method actors made everybody else on the screen look like they were phoning in their lines. They had studied the Stanislavski method at the Actors Studio off Broadway under Lee Strasberg, and they went through Hollywood like termites through Pinocchio. 'No need for grace and poses', wrote Stanislavski, 'don't mix rubber stamp movements with true action.' An actor should aim at being his role, inhabiting his character until his lines seemed inevitable. Stanislavski's teachings spread from Russia to the Marxist fringe theatres of America in the thirties, picked up a dash of Italian neo-realism, made an

uneasy peace with Hollywood's star system, and surfaced with a Sunday punch at the local cinema in the high street.

There were plenty of the new cats, but most of them never pulled a part that coincided with the hipster lifestyle. Neither Rod Steiger nor Lee J. Cobb leap to mind when Hip comes up, fine actors though they were. James Dean, articulate only in body English, had a lot of the moves but was cast inevitably as a seeker after love and acceptance.

Nevertheless, he seemed for a moment to be the next batter up to the plate. 'How can I lose? In one hand I got Marlon Brando yelling "Fuck you all", in the other Monty Clift asking "Please help me".' Dean posed with the bongo drums for publicity stills, and arrived at the studios astride the statutory motorbike. Brando was less than encouraging. 'Whyn't'cha wear somethin' else 'sides last year's suit?' he said, and handed on the address of his analyst.

Dean was a casualty of Hollywood's discovery of the teenager, a box-office bonanza before the whole love-me, understand-me bit flopped over into pop. As far as Hollywood was concerned, hipsters were low-riding jeans from wardrobe.

96

When Dean died in 1955, Paul Newman inherited his next two roles. Newman was lucky because both parts were about as alternative as Central Casting would go: the boxer and the psychotic. He played Rocky Graziano (Lester Young's hat features in the early gym sequences) in *Somebody Up There Likes Me*, and Billy The Kid in *The Left Handed Gun*. All the Method hallmarks are hung out like bunting – illiteracy, delinquency, the compass-swing of the body sensing before the brain, the fear of conformity, the odd stylization of emotion. 'Poor Mr Newman', wrote the *New York Times*, 'seems to be auditioning alternately for the Moscow Art Players and the Grand Ol' Opry, as he ambles about, brooding, grinning or mumbling endlessly.' Which pegged that paper as Phi Beta Kappa, forget it. Oddly enough, when Newman played a jazzman in *Paris Blues* it turned out to be disappointingly three-button Brooks Bros, and not a patch on the hipster's semiology of his pool shark in *The Hustler*, cutting contests around the nominated pockets and all.

In American cinema, the hipster comes into focus briefly, if at all. Stacy Keach could have been capable of sketching it had *Fat City* required it, and Jack Nicholson and Robert Duvall probably have it within their repertoire. Al Pacino has prowled around the perimeter but came near only on stage in David Mamet's *American Buffalo*. Why doesn't someone issue Dustin Hoffman with a horn? We forgive him *Lenny*.

It comes down to Robert De Niro, for now. As Johnny Boy, his entry in *Mean Streets* into Tony's bar, a chick on each arm, overcoat, stingy-brim hat, spearpoint shirt and, inexplicably, no trousers, is one of cinema's great breaks. This character moves to a hidden metronome; he wakes the neighbourhood by firing off his .38 into the night, yet spreads a handkerchief on the ground before sitting down. Even looking for Mafia acceptance, he is constitutionally bound to raise the ante to the maddest heights. Johnny Boy is a flipster, with hipster licks. *Raging Bull* gave him his inarticulate boxer with a vengeance. *New York, New York* saddled him with Liza Minnelli, but got the jazz obsession and the band bus right. Ralph Burns composed the music, and Georgie Auld advised on the tenor sax.

Of the younger actors, only Mickey Rourke looks like he knows the history of the free-wheeling night-crawler. His damaged hipster in Francis Coppola's *Rumblefish* stirred quite a few movie memories, and raised the ghost of a hope.

Top: *Paul Newman (*The Hustler*)*
Bottom: *Paul Newman and Everett Sloan (*Somebody Up There Likes Me*)*

Alan Ladd

JEEPERS PEEPERS

GATS, G-MEN AND GUNSELS

Way back in the fifties, when most kids were playing pirates in the streets, a few of us were busy looking for a pretend game where we could be amnesiacs trying to clear our names in twenty-four hours. We had been reading the pulps, those dime thrillers that seemed to have been published secondhand with a coffee-ring logo on the cover, a crushed crane-fly at the denouement, and half the bread back on return.

Since then, the great divide between culture and crap has silted over. You don't have to read pulp under the desk anymore because it's right up there on the blackboard. In fact, there's an academic industry around the novels of Dashiell Hammett, Raymond Chandler, James M. Cain, and Horace McCoy. John Franklin Bardin has made it into Penguin, and even Mickey Spillane is taught in the French universities. Can Hank *Slay Ride For Cutie* Janson be next?

Chandler and Hammett have been pretty much picked clean. The fancy which can tell you that Sherlock Holmes kept his nose candy in the toe of a Turkish slipper, can by now draw you a diagram of Philip Marlowe's or Sam Spade's office, complete with filing cabinet, fifth of rye in the second drawer, and back-to-front legend on the frosted glass door. Private eyes have their hip moments, but for the wild freewheeling imagination in the city of night, and more than a pinch of hipsters' paranoia, no one tops either Cornell Woolrich or David Goodis.

'DOWN THERE... was Eddie, behind the battered piano in Harriet's Hut, a rickety gin palace at the dark dead end of Skid Row. Life jolted Eddie from his dream – and he awoke in a wet back alley, standing over a dead man, with a knife in his hand.' That's the blurb for Goodis's *Down There* (filmed as *Shoot The Pianist* by François Truffaut), next to the advert for 'MEN – BE STRONGER!!!'

Dark Passage (a movie vehicle for Humphrey Bogart) centres on a convict on the run, undergoing plastic surgery to avoid recapture, but still taking time out to dig a little Swing. *Dragging at the cigarette he stooped over and began going through the record albums. When he came to Basie he frowned. There was a lot of Basie. The best Basie. The same Basie he liked. There was 'Every Tub' and 'Swinging The Blues' and 'Texas Shuffle'. There was 'John's Idea' and 'Lester Leaps In' and 'Out The Window'. He took a glance at the window. He came back to the records and decided to play 'Texas Shuffle'. He remembered that every time he played 'Texas Shuffle' he got a picture of countless steers parading fast across an endless plain in Texas. He switched on the current and got the record under the needle. 'Texas Shuffle' began to roll softly and it was very lovely. It clicked with the fact that he had a cigarette in his mouth, watching the smoke go up, and the police didn't know he was here.*

The good guys in Goodis dig jazz. The Basie fan's best friend is a trumpeter – or was, until someone beat his skull in with the trumpet. 'I put my entire attitude toward life into a trumpet riff. You told me it was cosmic-ray stuff. Something

Humphrey Bogart

Jack Nicholson

Lee Marvin

Robert Mitchum

Jack Webb

Dick Powell

Alain Delon

Kirk Douglas

from a billion miles away, bouncing off the moon, coming down and into my brain and coming out of my trumpet.'

Woolrich, like Goodis, started out as a 'serious' novelist and gave up to write at one-cent-a-word for the pulps. He wrote so much that he used a couple of aliases, William Irish and George Hopley, as well as his own name, and scores of movies were based on his psychological thrillers, including *Cat People*, *Rear Window*, *The Bride Wore Black* and *Phantom Lady*. In fact, the development of film noir – a shorthand term for morbidly pessimistic big city thrillers with low-slung lighting – owes as much to the pulps (and crime news photographer Weegee) as it does to Alan Ladd, Richard Widmark, Robert Mitchum, Richard Conte or Bogart.

The orderly world of cause and effect scarcely exists in this shadowed world, down among the losers where chance is sovereign. Innocent men are abruptly twisted into obsessional avengers by random blows of fate, and descend to the drifters' netherworld of cold-water walk-ups furnished with a mattress, a solitary chair, and a balefully flashing neon sign outside the window. The past is always painful or erased by some personal powercut, it is always night, and the plots jerk like a bebop line. Most thrillers roll out the mystery then roll

it back up like score paper. Woolrich wrote so fast and flying that, like a great gone alto saxophonist on his night, searing scene stacked on searing scene until conclusive conclusion was less likely than that the club-owner closed up at dawn.

As with the blues, bereavement is the normal condition. *Rendezvous In Black* cuts straight to the loaded dice as the hero's childhood sweetheart, waiting as ever under the clock for their regular date, is beheaded by a bottle flung from a passing plane. The amnesiac hero of *The Black Curtain* doesn't even know why he is being chased, but runs anyway, staring out in horror as a nightmare pursuer cracks the windows of a subway train in a fury of frustration as he eludes him. Ralph Ellison should write about Woolrich.

W.R. Burnett, famous for *Little Caesar*, *High Sierra* and *The Asphalt Jungle*, seems to have been one of the few thriller writers to understand the hipster. In *Vanity Row*, Bob Dumas, a piano player who earns his living playing Carmen Cavallero-type stuff at Cipriano's, but whose heart is in the black jazz joints, is hauled in by the cops as a murder suspect. Down at headquarters, he has a problem making himself understood.

Look Captain. The point with me is music. Not wars, not boffs, not who shot who and why. I'll tell you a story. You may get THIS one. A couple of musicians were walking past St Dominic's Cathedral. Something happened up above and that great goddam heavy bell came crashing down on the sidewalk making a hell of a racket – enough to scare a man out of his wits. One of the musicians yelled: 'What in the Jesus was that?' And the other one said: 'E flat.'

The low budget and lower lighting B films that sprang from the pulps reached for jazz to establish the 'round midnight' mood. Countless forgotten thrillers spilled sax solos over the neon reflected on the wet sidewalks – Illinois Jacquet in *DOA*, Eddie Heywood in *The Dark Corner*, Shorty Rogers in *The Big Combo*.

The death of the black-and-white poverty row B movie spelt the end of the great age of film noir, and today's best thriller writers like Elmore Leonard and George V. Higgins specialize in dialogue, not atmosphere. Nobody's doing anything but thinking angles in their world . . .

NIGHTHAWKS

THE BEATS

'San Francisco' says Kenneth Rexroth, poet, scholar, elder statesman of dissent, 'is the only city in the United States which was not settled overland by the westward-spreading puritan tradition, or by the Walter Scott, fake-cavalier tradition of the South.'

Frisco resisted incorporation. Its literature was at variance with the prevailing patterns, maintaining closer links with London and Paris than with the Jewish-Angst-dominated New York. Intellectually, it drew upon a tradition of dissent stretching right back to the Red thirties. Wobblies, conscientious objectors and anarchists had all found sanctuary in the Mediterranean atmosphere of *laissez-faire*.

The city looks across the Pacific to Asia. Chinese and Japanese have settled here too, their Buddhist and Zen Buddhist temples emanating gentle ripples of contemplation, pacifism and self-discovery. And it was in this city of hills that the Silent Generation of the fifties – demoralized by the Korean War, disgusted by the craven passivity of their elders before the denunciations of Senator Joe McCarthy, and living in the shadow of The Bomb – found their voice.

The Beats who first hung around Greenwich Village had plenty of disgust, but no real alternative to the society that they rejected. Only when Ginsberg and Kerouac hit San Francisco did things begin to focus. Rexroth organized one of

103

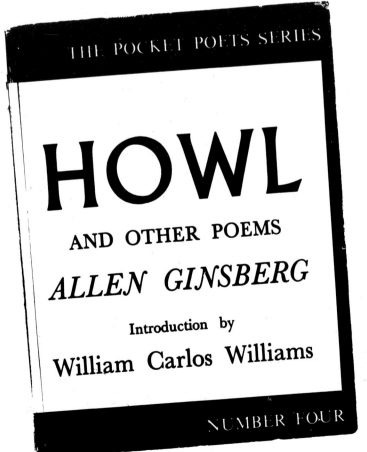

his frequent public poetry readings at the Six Gallery, and this time the results were explosive.

Ginsberg read *Howl*.

I saw the best minds of my generation destroyed by
madness, starving hysterical naked,
dragging themselves through the negro streets at dawn
looking for an angry fix,
angelheaded hipsters burning for the ancient heavenly
connection to the starry dynamo in the machinery
of night.

It landed on the audience with the impact of an Old Testament prophecy. The Beat Generation was up and running. San Francisco became the centre of the new do-it-yourself poetry renaissance; clubs, cellars, coffee bars jumped with talent. Lawrence Ferlinghetti, proprietor of the spearheading City Lights bookstore (shelves of Celine, Genet, Henry Miller, Nelson Algren), publisher and poet, said, 'My whole kick has been oral poetry. The poets today are talking to themselves. They have no other audience. We're trying to capture an audience.'

And they did. From San Francisco, the Beat movement spread south to Venice West and back east to New York. Jack Kerouac became a one-man Chamber of Commerce to North Beach, the barker on the low rent scene. His first

novel, *The Town And The City*, was published in 1950, but he had to wait until 1957 for a publisher to accept *On The Road*. He had written it over an eight-year period from 1948, capturing precisely the coast-to-coast restlessness of the hipster, the overdrive exuberance and the ravenous appetite for experience. It wasn't writing, it was typing, commented the publishing establishment, illustrating the gulf between the square world and the hip.

'The only people for me are the mad ones, the ones who are mad to live, mad to talk, mad to be saved, desirous of everything at the same time, the ones who never yawn or say a commonplace thing, but burn, burn, burn like fabulous roman candles' (Dean Moriarty, hero of *On The Road*).

Kerouac's spiritual desperation crash-coursed him through Zen, Roman Catholicism, mysticism and hip. Drugs, sex and jazz fuelled the hot-rod go-go-go prose style because only they were spontaneous enough and defiant enough and high-octane enough to keep it on the move. 'I

want God to show me his face!' yelled the writer, blasting frenetically up and down the map of America. After the success of *On The Road*, his books burst through the dam in a rush; *The Subterraneans*, *The Dharma Bums*, *Doctor Sax*, *Maggie Cassidy*, *Visions Of Cody* and *Mexico City Blues* were published within a year. 'My work', he said, 'comprises one vast book like Proust's, except that my remembrances are written on the run.'

There were critics and disciples. Norman Podhoretz was less than gassed. 'What you get in these books is a man proclaiming that he is alive and offering every trivial experience he has ever had in evidence.' Seymour Krim ('Shake It For The World, Smartass') dug it, however. 'It was actual communication from living soul to swinging living soul, and nuts to all outdated formal restraints and laughable writing conventions, all so pitiably irrelevant and IN THE WAY.'

How are we to live? 'This generation cannot conceive of

the question in any but personal terms', said John Clellon Holmes, author of *The Horn*, a hipster's view of the tragic disintegration of saxophonist Edgar Pool, a loose mixture of Charlie Parker and Lester Young. The answer was solipsism, an assertion of the self as the centre of the universe. In the poem, a return to the first person singular of Walt Whitman, and in the novel the supremacy of the commentator, digging everything, singing the body electric.

But Kerouac's salvation scheme burned him out, and he ended his days back with his mother. The hipster pulse passed to Ken Kesey, who wrote *One Flew Over The Cuckoo's Nest* and *Sometimes A Great Notion* before deciding to spend his royalties on a busload of acid freaks. 'I'd rather be a lightning rod than a seismograph', he told Tom Wolfe. Neal Cassady, the original for Kerouac's hipster, signed on for the trip as an heirloom from The Beats. 'He will answer all questions, although not exactly in that order, because we can't stop here, next rest area 40 miles, you understand, spinning off memories, metaphors, literary, oriental, hip allusions, all punctuated by the unlikely expression "you understand", wrote Wolfe in *The Electric Kool-Aid Acid Test*. Cassady dropped dead beside the railroad tracks in Mexico, before his forty-second birthday, and Kerouac a year later at forty-seven.

Norman Mailer took more than a passing interest in the phenomenon of the hipster. 'The White Negro', typically preoccupied with existentialism and the orgasm, still observed that jazz had made a 'knifelike entrance into culture', that 'Hip is the sophistication of the wise primitive in a giant jungle', and that 'Hip is pretty.' He also made a list, intended as 'a primitive foray into the more formal aspects of Hip'. Instinct was Hip, logic was Square; midnight was Hip, noon was Square; a catlike walk from the hip was Hip, a bearlike walk from the shoulders was Square; Thelonious Monk was Hip, Dave Brubeck was Square. The inventory comes unstuck in places: Nixon was Hip, and Dulles Square. Now's the time, Norman!

All this theorizing is blown clear away by the black novelist, Ralph Ellison. The hero of *Invisible Man* has taken refuge from the hostile world in a cellar, tapped into Monopolated Light & Power to illuminate with 1,369 bulbs his despair, and sits it out with his Louis Armstrong records. 'Who knows but that, on the lower frequencies, I speak for you?'

Loud and clear, Mr Ellison. Loud and clear.

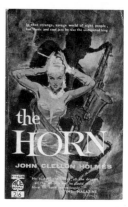

"*Brew Moore pays little attention to anyone, he drinks his beer, he gets loaded and eye-heavy, but he never misses a beat or a note, because music is his heart, and in music he has found that pure message to give the world — only trouble is, they don't understand.*"   Jack Kerouac.

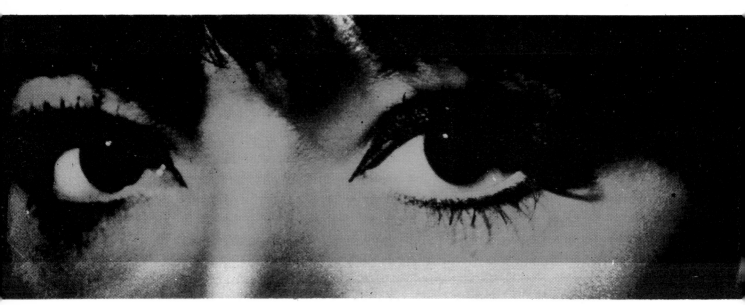

Greco

EXISTENTIALIST A GO GO

'People imagined that I used to make love to Jean-Paul Sartre on marble tables in bistros, even though marble is very cold,' admits chanteuse Juliette Greco who, as one of the existentialist philosopher's 'enchanted circle', helped detonate a middle-class youthquake that shattered the strict moral traditions of the post-war French.

It was the overtly-romanticized era of the bereted Beatnik, slinky Bohemian and open-toed sandal which flourished, from the early forties until Sartre upped and moved on in 1962, in the Saint Germain des Pres district of

Paris. A Left-Bank literati movement which drastically re-evaluated politics, art, music, movies and sexual mores.

Possessed of a black Balmain dress ('a blackboard on which audiences gave full rein to their imagination'), Gallic cheekbones, a high-profile friendship with Brando and a deep nicotine-nurtured voice that emphasized the explicit lyrics she enacted, Greco – as with Brigitte Bardot – was not only a symbol of postwar youth, but physical evidence of the sexual freedom and hard-won independence that Simone de Beauvoir had boldly campaigned for in *Le Deuxième Sexe* and, likewise, Françoise Sagan in *Bonjour Tristesse*.

'I was not exactly innocent of the image that people had of me', Greco later reflected. 'I was an object of scandal, but only because I was normal. I experienced women's liberation in a completely natural way a long time before people talked about it.'

In cahoots with fast-living novelist Boris Vian, singers Catherine Sauvage, Yves Montand, Jacques Brel and Georges Brassens, movie stars Gerard Philipe and Simone Signoret and New Wave directors Chabrol, Resnais, Truffaut and Vadim, Greco's talents illuminated the clubs and cafés of Saint Germain.

Almost a city within a city – and once a French Resistance stronghold – the progressive community still felt threatened by reactionaries who branded them faddish, decadent... even unpatriotic.

The Gauloise-hazed Le Tabou cellar club ('the true sanctuary of a new generation') and later Club Saint Germain des Pres and Le Rose Rouge were hole-in-the-wall havens where – fifteen years prior to flower power – the Dark Angel Greco perfected her *persona* performing protest songs and where Parisiennes also indulged their obsession with Black American jazz.

Club Saint Germain des Pres quickly established itself as Europe's premier jazz room – later sharing the accolade with The Blue Note.

If Greco was 'the muse of Saint Germain', Brigitte Bardot would soon become its most celebrated personality. It was BB's failure to launch a vocal career that prompted her to concentrate on movies and, in Vadim's *And God Created Woman...*, she emerged as the celluloid manifestation of both the de Beauvoir and Sagan role model – a fearless, independently-minded woman free to choose her sexual lifestyle in a society still intent on suppressing such ideals.

Come 1962 and many of Saint Germain's most creative denizens were dead or scattered. An era ended and the couturiers moved in. The sweet smell of excess being replaced by the reek of chic and the wistful Françoise Hardy – Courrège boots and pelmet-curtain hair – became Paree's Beat-Age 'Yeh-Yeh-Yeh' girl.

Bardot

RACKET JACKETS

SLICK SLEEVES
AND COOL COVERS

Plenty of record companies caught the sound, but only Clef, Blue Note and Contemporary were the labels where the *sleeves* were happenin' too. Norman Granz was the first entrepreneur to employ quality artwork as opposed to photographic mug-shots to sleeve much of his Clef product and, to this end, hired Chicago's own David Stone Martin, whom he first met when they were both associated with Asch Records.

David Stone Martin has to be the most gifted illustrator ever to have turned his attention to the jazz world and successfully translated the vigour, the wit and drama inherent in the music. For some, a David Stone Martin sleeve became just as important to the purchaser as the music – be it Bird, Lady Day, Prez or a Jazz at The Phil jam – it protected. The simple line drawings, the splash of colour, the ability to both recognize and focus on a specific gesture, stance or characteristic, his fascination with hands – these were all quickly seized upon by an entire generation of late fifties European art-school students (most notably in Britain), amongst whom David Stone Martin's influence reigned unchallenged. To this day, his finest work remains without equal.

Stateside, it was different. In the same manner as saxmen vainly attempted to cop Bird's best licks, similarly, third-rate talents blatantly tried to pass off their inferior scribbles as Stone Martin-styled. Those bereft of any self-esteem even signed their work in the manner of the Great Man. Martin laughs, 'It's something that happens and you can't fight it.' When, in the mid-forties, Granz set up his own highly successful operation, Martin became a permanent fixture – a ten year-plus partnership during which, Martin estimates, he created well in excess of 200 sleeve designs. Seemingly, it was Mo Asch and photographer/moviemaker Gjon Mili who convinced Granz that to sleeve his records in Martin's designs not only made commercial sense, but was artistically sound.

In producing a folio of what amounts to some of America's finest contemporary art, Martin avoided working in isolation with only an advance test-pressing for reference. 'I worked with Granz in the environment of the musician – many of whom I knew very well. So, that was the canvas – mutual agreement.'

Vanity being what it is, Martin claims that not even the most volatile of Clef Records' performers ever took exception to the manner in which he portrayed them. 'Quite the contrary – they approved of what I did. Charlie Parker . . . Billie Holiday . . . they understood what I was striving to achieve.'

Acclaimed in other spheres of creative design – art director of war information and illustrating *Time* magazine covers, to cite just two – Martin admits that he is especially satisfied with the work he created for Granz. Of these, Martin maintains a personal fondness for the paintings that decorate Billie Holiday's recordings.

Now, in his seventies, David Stone Martin still remains very active. In the early 1980s he acquired a Japanese patron who, to date, has commissioned sixty portraits of various jazz greats for his private collection.

If DSM transformed the browser bin into a street-smart art gallery, similarly, Reid Miles turned Blue Note sleeves into a running commentary on all that was innovative in post-war graphic design. Founded in 1939, by Alfred Lion, and later joined by Francis Wolff, Blue Note Records were distinguished by three days of paid rehearsals and the best sound engineer on the scene – Rudy Van Gelder. This pursuit of excellence extended to the packaging. In 1956, the Lion and the Wolff hired designer Miles, who went on to turn out over 500 definitively stylish covers. Whether trimming Wolff's photos into near-abstract gestures and adorning them with a one-colour tint, or jamming the typography into a bebop slipstream, Miles had unfailing grease.

Much the same can be said of Lester Koenig's LA-based Contemporary label. It was not only the first jazz label to introduce 45 rpm singles, stereo and attain national distribution, but was also an independent outfit that cared as much for the presentation of its wares as Blue Note. Indeed, the winning combination of lensman William Claxton's couture-styled compositions and the bold, brightly coloured lettering of Tri-Arts studio positively oozed cool California chic.

Three decades on, these sleeves continue to inspire, tantalize, but mostly elude a new generation of illustrators attempting to reverse into the future.

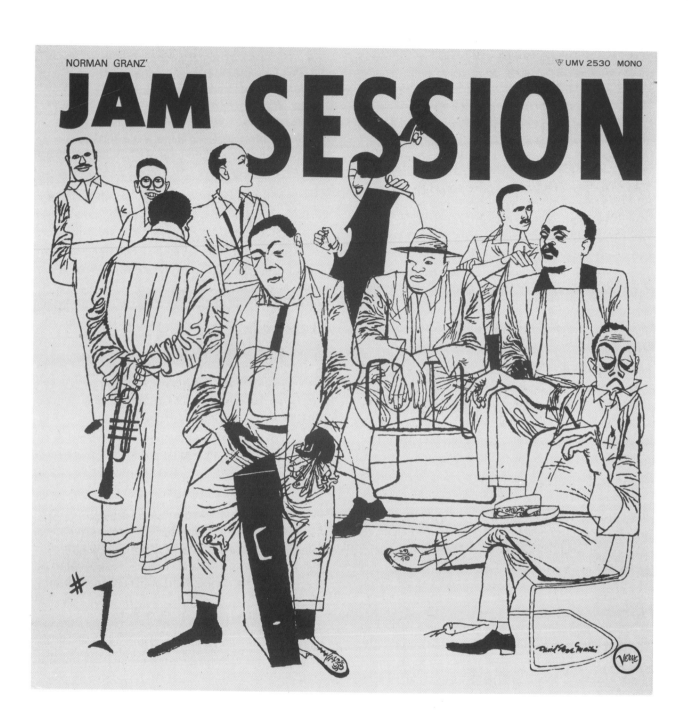

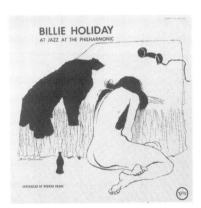

115

APRIL 27, 1961   35¢

down beat

THE BI-WEEKLY MUSIC MAGAZINE

SPOTLIGHT ON THE BIG BANDS

117

JOHNNY GRIFFIN
THE CONGREGATION
BLUE NOTE 1580

47 WEST 63rd STREET

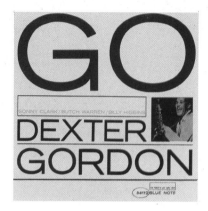

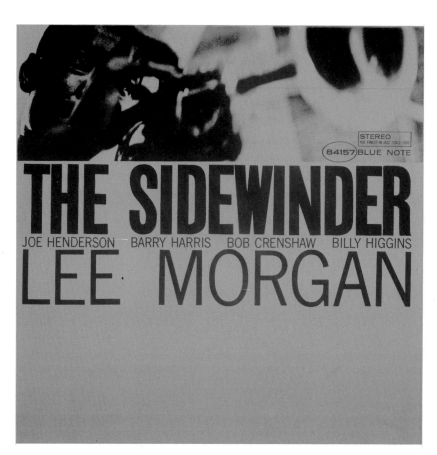

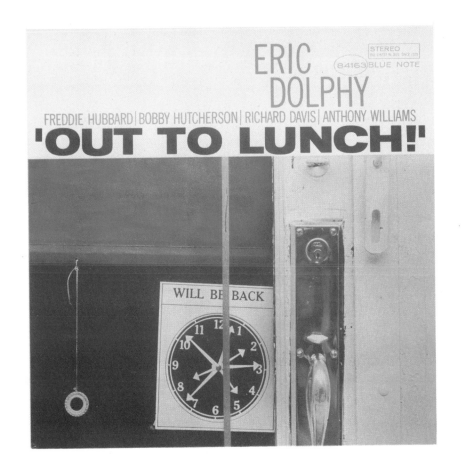

ERIC
DOLPHY

FREDDIE HUBBARD | BOBBY HUTCHERSON | RICHARD DAVIS | ANTHONY WILLIAMS

'OUT TO LUNCH!'

STEREO
84163 BLUE NOTE

WILL BE BACK

LEE MORGAN
WITH HANK MOBLEY / KENNY RODGERS / HORACE SILVER
PAUL CHAMBERS / CHARLIE PERSIP   BLUE NOTE 1541

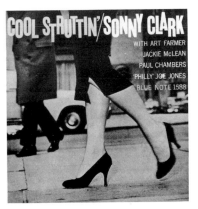

COOL STRUTTIN'/SONNY CLARK
WITH ART FARMER
JACKIE McLEAN
PAUL CHAMBERS
'PHILLY JOE JONES
BLUE NOTE 1588

THE
INCREDIBLE
WITH GRANT GREEN & DONALD BAILEY   JIMMY
SMITH
"I'M MOVIN' ON"

Contemporary C3509: Howard Rumsey's Lighthouse All-Stars * Barney Kessel * Hampton Hawes' Trio *with* Shelly Manne

LIGHTHOUSE AT LAGUNA

CONTEMPORARY

8481 MELROSE PLACE • LOS ANGI

RECORDS

S 46, CALIFORNIA

TOM WAITS
FOR NO MAN

In an iodine-yellow spotlight beside a gas pump, the singer grips the mike stand like a rumdum adhering to railings. He's wearing a mismatched black suit that pinches under the arms, too-short sleeves that expose the wrist bones, and a stingy-brim hat. His corncrake voice prowls the thickets of 'Tom Traubert's Blues', low, so low you catch only one word in three, sibilants hissing like air leaking from tyres.

> *Now the dogs are barking*
> *And the taxi cabs parking,*
> *A lot they can do for me.*

Tom Waits casts a spell like nobody else. He's all the great American losers rolled into one – 'I don't care who I hafta step on on my way back down', he cracks. There isn't much of today in the image. Time, which waits for no man, has waited for Tom Waits, and he has ransacked the history of his country's grifters, panhandlers, no-hopers, knock-nutty boxers who still come on as The Kid, barflies and bloodbank

regulars to furnish the pavement-coloured landscape of his mind.

Kerouac, Nelson Algren, bar-room and barrack songs, the Great American Loneliness of Edward Hopper's paintings – 'Nighthawks', 'Second Storey Sunlight', 'Two on the Aisle', 'Hotel by a Railroad', like that – and the burnt-out end of vaudeville lives. It's a losing hand of influences so far as mass popularity is concerned, but it gives him a living, fuels his imagination for some of the best lyric writing today, and has garnered him secure cult status. 'Yeah', he growls, rubbing the back of his head like a drunk trying to find the fingerholes in a bowling ball, 'Marcel Marceau gets more airplay than I do. Heard myself once in North Dakota, that's all.'

He started out singing his own songs at The Troubadour in LA in 1972, after scuffling variously as a lavatory attendant, dishwasher, fireman, truck-driver – 'I was a jack-off of all trades' – and doorman. His first album was entitled *Closing Time*. He's always been an acquired taste, but the hip acquired it. He played the Palookaville circuit to start – beer-bars, roadhouses – graduated to the jazz clubs – Ronnie Scott's, The Montmartre – rose to the grander auditoriums, without shedding an ounce of that intimate,

after-hours feel. 'I get run down on the road. Get tired of myself, usually wanna get twelve hours of sleep and some twelve-year-old scotch. The uncontrollable urge to play Iowa has finally left me.'

In recent years he has acted and written film scores, mainly for Francis Coppola, doing both in *Rumblefish*, contributing ideas and music for *One From The Heart*, and playing the manager in *Cotton Club*. His best albums, *Foreign Affairs*, *Small Change*, *Swordfishtrombones*, and *Rain Dogs*, field enough atmosphere and characters for a raft of black-and-white B movies. He has written lines like 'Small Change got rained on with his own .38, and no one's gone over to close his eyes.' Sadder and tighter they don't come. He watched a lot of dreams die along Sunset Boulevard.

'It takes all you can muster to just drown out the sirens every night. I don't see much hope. Can't go any further West. The girls still come from like Nebraska and stuff, go out there, you know, wanna be in pictures. They end up on their backs in one of the rooms.' And here we go, down 'n' dirty for the 'step right up, Little Egypt' bump 'n' grind. These days, he has quit LA for New York, and – more significantly – given up cigarettes. It's hard to think of him

healthy. If ever a performer epitomized the old Harry 'the Hipster' Gibson injunction, 'Let's smoke up the joint so a man can breathe', it's Tom Waits.

As he talks, shoulders up like one of those collar-up Depression shiverers atop the spine of a transcontinental B&O freight train, hands moving in carny's mysterioso, voice barely crossing the threshold of speech, you feel like you're eavesdropping on a flophouse airshaft. 'I twist whatever I see, you know. Most of my writing is a metaphor for something else. Just add my own funhouse mirror.'

He keeps hip company – Teddy Edwards or Herb Hardesty on tenor, Jack Sheldon on trumpet, Shelly Manne on drums – and plays his own mean mission hall piano. And you'd have to go back to Louis Armstrong to find pipes likes Tom's.

Smellin like a brewery
Lookin like a tramp
Ain't got a quarter
Got a postage stamp
And a five o'clock shadow boxing
All around the town
Talking with the old men
Sleeping on the ground
Bazanti bootin
Al zootin al hoot
And Al Cohn
Sharin this apartment
With a telephone pole . . .

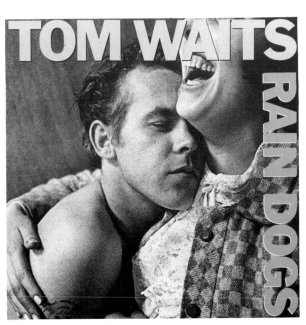

127

LES NOUVEAUX BOHEMIANS

That hipness doesn't come off the peg crushes the conceit of those whose career is dependent only upon the cut of their trousers.

Pop hopefuls in search of a style (and a purpose) frequently rummage through the jazz warehouse, trying on the berets, the zoots or that all-purpose little black cocktail dress. Though silk-suited soulsters endeavour to keep the faith, when left to its own devices, pop has come up with little greasier than psychedelic silliness and chaps in frocks.

Colin MacInnes laid it out when he dropped his manifesto into *Absolute Beginners*:

That brings me to today, and to the third item in my education, my university, you might say, and that's the jazz clubs. Now, you can think what you like about the art of jazz – quite frankly, I don't care what you think, because jazz is a thing so wonderful that if anybody doesn't rave about it, all you can feel for them is pity: not that I'm making out I really understand it all – I mean, certain LPs leave me speechless. But the great thing about the jazz world and all the kids that enter into it, is that no one, not a soul, cares what your class is, or what your race is, or what your income, or if you're a boy, or girl, or bent, or versatile, or what you are – so long as you dig the scene and behave yourself, and have left all that crap behind you, too, when you come in the jazz club door. The result of all this is that, in the jazz world, you meet all kinds of cats, on absolutely equal terms, who can clue you up

in all kinds of directions – in social directions, in culture directions, in sexual directions, and in racial directions...in fact, almost anywhere, really, you want to go to learn.

Such gifted mavericks as Rickie Lee Jones and Tom Waits find a genuine affinity for the hipster lifestyle, eschewing pop's otherwise self-imposed restrictions. 'Our writing and singing styles have nothing in common,' said Rickie Lee. 'But we walk around the same streets, and I guess it's primarily a jazz-motivated situation for both of us. We're living on the jazz side of life, the other side of the tracks, and it's real insecure, constant improvisation.'

The quest for the Holy Grail of Hip is predominantly a British obsession. For the successors of MacInnes' fifties teenager, Beatlemania was strictly for the birds. In *Mod* London, the latest Jimmy Smith Blue Note import casually tucked under the left arm was as essential to one's ongoing status as the width of the knitted slim jim, length of a jacket vent or the depth of shine on the college loafers.

Above all, Georgie Fame walked it like he talked it. Semi-resident at London's Flamingo Club, Fame worked to capacity crowds of Mohair Mods and black US servicemen, blending Jimmy Smith, Mose Allison, Motown, R&B, vocalese, blue beat, hard bop and Madras cotton band jackets into a lifestyle soundtrack.

Rod 'The Mod' Stewart's first press handout revealed an ambition to sing with Count Basie, but it was Georgie who clocked that one up.

Cats didn't come much cooler than this 21-year-old who not only topped the UK singles chart (Dec 1964) with a rework of Jon Hendricks' 'Yeh Yeh', but on his first studio album, included everything from 'The Monkey Time' to 'Moody's Mood For Love'.

For a brief moment, it looked like a re-run of the forties when jazz and pop sat cheek-to-cheek on the charts: Herman beside Haymes, Kenton beside King Cole.

Jazz made one of its great leaps forward in the late fifties, however, outstripping dance and, as it turned out, most of its public. The revolution engineered by Cecil Taylor, Ornette Coleman, and later, Albert Ayler, Archie Shepp, Pharaoh Sanders, Anthony Braxton and the Art Ensemble Of Chicago, destroyed any possibility of a consensus of pop and jazz tastes. Jazz was still the musical cutting edge, but pop was now saddled with a ten to fifteen-year assimilation period. British punk took all of that to surface after jazz's nihilistic

Europe's finest modern jazz rendezvous.....

JEFF KRUGER'S JAZZ AT THE *Flamingo*

33-37 Wardour St., W.1

Open every WEDNESDAY - FRIDAY - SATURDAY - SUNDAY 7.30-11 p.m.

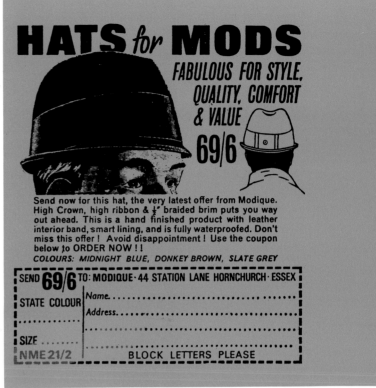

New Wave had reared up to the accompaniment of burning ghettos.

But jazz New Wave licks did eventually find their way into pop's vocabulary. Captain Beefheart, Ian Dury, Robert Wyatt, James Chance and a handful of others hit on the screams and scrambles.

Reminiscent of the early fifties, when sidemen from the bands of Duke and The Count often cut the most raucous of rock records, the pop fraternity regularly recruits jazz giants for its studio sessions.

Whereas, it was once pop's best kept secret, later, The Beatles, The Rolling Stones, Scott Walker, David Sylvian, Matt Bianco and Elvis Costello made much of the fact they requisitioned the jazz clout of masters like Ronnie Scott, Sonny Rollins, Evan Parker, Kenny Wheeler, Ronnie Ross and Chet Baker for their albums.

Policeman Sting bought the whole enchillada.

For *The Dream Of The Blue Turtle*, he assembled a working unit of Branford Marsalis and Kenny Kirkland from the prestigious Wynton Marsalis Band and the rhythm team of Darryl 'The Munch' Jones and Omar Hakim from Miles Davis and Weather Report.

Replying to jazz slumming snipes, Sting said: 'I ended up with these musicians because I thought that they were the best players, and also because the way they related to me and to each other seemed *right*.'

Few musicians in any field approach their work with such care as the enigmatic Van Morrison. Openly critical of the slapdash greedheads of pop, he's closer to someone like Louis Jordan, honing his songs with a working road band. Hit singles don't figure much in his thinking, and he has shelved more album projects than he's actually released.

In the early eighties, the kids rediscovered jazz. Even though figures like Michael Jackson outsell the entire jazz history catalogue, fine, straight ahead youngsters like trumpet player Wynton Marsalis and Stanley Jordan not only found respectable levels of pop-like stature but established themselves as role models.

Meanwhile, the latest crop of Brit pop bands to give more than a nod towards the flexibility offered by jazz include The Style Council, Working Week, Everything But The Girl and Sade.

Jazz aspects that have appeal range from the fringe – Getz/Gilberto bossa nova and Julie London – to deep dish Blue Note hard bop, Billie Holiday, Cu-Bop and Jimmy Smith.

Though Elvis Costello and Joe Jackson gravitate towards a more rock 'n' soul stance, they prefer to wear their influences on their (album) sleeves, while endorsing their music with indelible signatures. To Costello's credit, he brings to pop music an artistic sensibility equal to that of the great jazz innovators.

With the advent of video, image stylists become as important to the performer as songwriters. Distinguishing the difference between the participants in pop music videos and fashion house commercials can be impossible. Both appear to be implementing the same sales pitch. Never was this more apparent when, in 1986, Sam Cooke's 'Wonderful World' soundtrack for a Levi's 501/TV commercial lifted Cooke postumously to his highest ever UK chart position.

Sade is perhaps the one person to have utilized this situation to her advantage – the lady's haute couture expertise enabling her to project the ultimate ritzy fantasy.

Nefertiti profile and smoky siren call are caressed by yearning skyscraper sax and gently brushed rhythm to create a soft-focus illusion of ultimate sophistication for the unsophisticated.

Hers is the winning three gold bars across combination: right person, right place, right commodity that claimed a six

The Selling of Sade

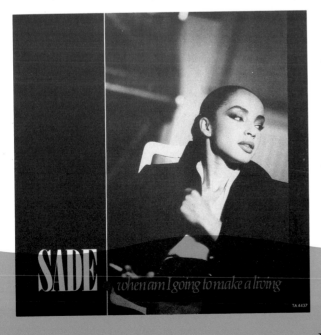

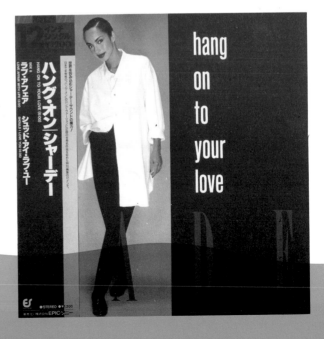

John Lurie
Solo Saxophone

Carnegie Recital Hall   154 West 57 Street
8:30 PM   Thursday, July 3, 1980
Balcony $6.00   Orchestra $6.50

Stan Getz and Astrud Gilberto

million plus selling jackpot with the *Diamond Life* debut. Sade is a sable-fable, a Cartier-inspired dream. She's the tapered ankle about to step from the chauffeured Daimler.

Comparisons between Sade and Lady Day are a must to avoid.

Yet, at the same time, her label-mate Alison Moyet (*Alf*), who had latched on to Billie Holiday's 1944 recording of 'That Old Devil Called Love', was taking her version of the song to the top of the UK singles chart. Ironically, making the charts was something that Lady Day failed to accomplish, even posthumously.

But it's not just Brits who have veered towards jazz when released from rock's starting-gate. The list of Americans who have dug in is equally impressive, equally thought-provoking in its ways, whys and wherefores. Tom Waits, Rickie Lee Jones, Ben Sidran and John Lurie, can be excused the line-up. Theirs has always been the world of the truly cool, where songs come equipped with scratched videos compiled from old Movietone newsreels.

Others include Chaka Khan, Michael Franks, Donald Fagen (both as soloist and Steely Dan mainstay), David Byrne, Joni Mitchell, August Darnell aka Kid Creole, Was (Not Was), Carly Simon, Kenny Rankin – all are among those who have, at one point, swapped pop for the rough riff or the poignant pull of a 52nd Street-era roll-up.

Mainly, these cats are white. Black musicians assume hipness to be a natural birthright. They've rarely been adept at looking back in order to view the future. Still, the occasional nods are there. Gil Scott-Heron's 'John Coltrane and Lady Day' pays dues and respect. Likewise, Stevie Wonder has penned his tribute 'Sir Duke' and jammed on a Dizzy Gillespie album. Chaka Khan also notched a Diz-date, musically-canoodling up to the trumpeter on a version of 'A Night In Tunisia' that incorporates Bird's celebrated four-bar break which has been grafted on direct from the actual Dial recording.

Dizzy re-enacted the very same role on Manhattan Transfer's shot at this bop standard. Thus, hipness is achieved by association. Robert Reisner once said of Charlie Parker that 'Bird was the supreme hipster. He made his own laws. His arrogance was enormous, his humility profound.'

Maybe Khan hoped hip rubs off. Maybe the whole deal was merely producer Arif Mardin hoping to re-create a time when questions didn't have to be asked about credibility. Who knows?

Manhattan Transfer are among the most blatant of the

135

mighty whiteys who have hopped to hip. They've groove-checked the right records and, clotheswise, shopped to shape. Somehow, while few will deny the group's musical expertise as they swap easily from doo-wop to bebop, Hauser and his gang pan out as no more than talented dilettantes, missing out on the truth. One stage palm tree never made a re-run of *Casablanca* – or, 'Little Egypt'.

Better is one-time Steve Miller Band pianist Ben Sidran's now-you-hear-funk-now-you-don't approach, which clips in to the sound of Mose Allison, come-on-and-get-that-church and even hard bop. It's instinctive rather than painfully constructed.

Sidran knows. In his book *Black Talk*, an engrossing and intelligent treatise on black music and black culture, he remembers that the term 'hippie' was used way back in the forties as a term of derision for the false or pseudo-hipster. In a world where originals flourish, fakes – however well disguised – are easy to spot.

In some ways, it was pointless Linda Ronstadt re-inventing herself as gift-wrapped candy for her *What's New* and *Lush Life* albums. True, they made money. True they re-established Ronstadt as a chart contender. But it was an empty victory. Not even the distinctive arrangements of Nelson Riddle could disguise the fact that the singer didn't understand the material on the music-stand. Peggy Lee or, for that matter, most Holiday Inn lounge singers would have outphrased her in their sleep.

Joni Mitchell, undoubtedly, is aware. It's not that she has the nous to employ such musicians as Jaco Pastorius, Wayne Shorter and Pat Metheny as sidemen – Carly Simon's choice of Phil Woods, Eddie Gomez, Grady Tate, Marty Paich, etc., didn't entirely rescue her *Torch* from a critical mauling – but rather that in her jazz involvement she's become an innovator rather than the imitator she was when Man-Tranning out of affection for Lambert, Hendricks and Ross ('They were *my* Beatles').

Charles Mingus, no hearing-aid volume-knob twiddler when it came to tuning into original sounds, handed out his own form of Grammy when he penned a series of songs specifically for Mitchell as one of his last earthly acts.

'This', Mingus was suggesting, 'is the way to go – the way that makes sense.' It didn't give the bassist the kind of pop credibility that he now enjoys – British youth, at least, was already au fait with the pop potential of 'Goodbye Pork Pie Hat' and the contents of *Ah Um* and *Oh, Yeah!* many years

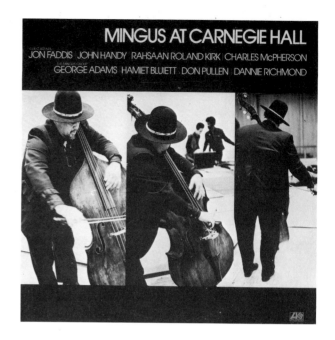

Rock is taking over what I did twenty years ago.

– Charles Mingus (1978)

136

Charlie Mingus

Hunt Emerson's Jazz Funnies

L'homme De Harlem

Japanese Jazz Comic

ago – but as a nudge it may have worked, belatedly, in his favour.

Much the same can be said of Raashan Roland Kirk and Thelonious Monk. Rip, Rig and Panic named themselves after the Kirk composition, whilst the *Downbeat* international critics award for best album of 1984 went to *That's The Way I Feel* – a two-record Monk tribute featuring such diverse contributors as Carla Bley, Joe Jackson, Dr John, Todd Rundgren, Johnny Griffin, Donald Fagen, Bobby McFerrin, NRBQ, Steve Lacy and Was (Not Was).

The last-named aggregation, a loosely-knit collection of funksters, metal merchants and jazzateers given shape by Detroit 'brothers' Don and David Was provided what many felt was the ultimate in mutant sound. In fashioning their *Born To Laugh At Tornadoes* album, a record that played host to obscene, live chicken-head muncher Ozzy Osbourne and early Detroit sweat-rocker Mitch Ryder, they clothed it in what they called 'a time proof suit' by having Branford Marsalis blow a righteous sax fade on Knack-man Doug Fieger's cut, while Mel Torme was persuaded to convert a black comedy ballad 'Zaz Turned Blue' into a moment of poignancy. All very odd. All very acceptable.

There will always be pop artists to impersonate the externals of the jazz style: some warmly, some with dollar-directed gaze.

Kid Creole owes his rise to an acid-tinged re-vamp of Cab Calloway in his Cotton Club days. The Lounge Lizards' John Lurie has eyes for a cinematique merger of Brando, Bernstein and Be-Bop.

On most it doesn't look good.

Even so, the donning of sharp suits and the slicking down of the rug continues as does pop's pursuit through the known past in anticipation of uncovering something that will last not only through the brevity of the present but a thread to hang on to as eternity beckons.

So, as the French and Japanese publish jazz comic strips, Ford's use a Monk soundtrack to sell family saloons, Miles Davis waxes Michael Jackson, Cyndi Lauper and Chaka Khan tunes, and Lester Bowie covers Sting, the circle turns full circle.

Pop makes money, but jazz makes the running.

In the words of Duke Ellington: 'From where it is, music is mostly all right, or at least in a healthy state for the future – in spite of the fact that it may sound as though it is being held hostage.'

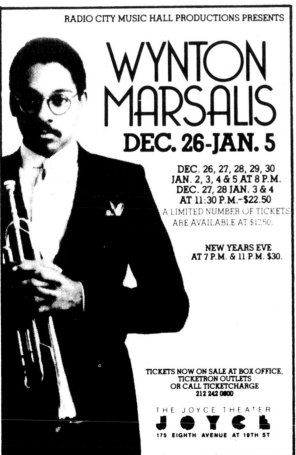

BERET CHIC
THE UNCRUSHABLE LID

Chic Beret

Miles Davis

Robert De Niro

Michelle Morgan

Dietrich

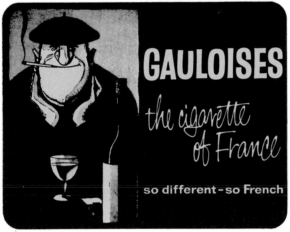

GAULOISES

the cigarette
of France

so different - so French

Dick Gregory

Lauren Bacall

Lana Turner

Faye Dunaway

Diz

MACHITO
And His Afro-Cubans

ACKNOWLEDGEMENTS

The Authors humbly doff the beret to all the following friends and organizations without whose generous assistance – and seemingly inexhaustible patience – this endeavour would never have come about.

Roger Armstrong, Jonas Bernhold, Roy Burchell, Art Blakey, Stan Britt, Martin Brown, Ted Carroll, John Cassavetes, Richard Cook, Ed Dipple, John Fenton, Bob Fisher, Slim Gaillard, Andy Gill, Jayne Houghton, Bullmoose Jackson, Nick Kennedy, Andrew Lauder, Dave Lewis, David Stone Martin, Tony Middleton, Jonathan Morrish, Dennis Munday, Johnny Otis, Rob Partridge, Harold & Barbara Pendleton, Ian Ralfini, Judith Riley, Shorty Rogers, Horace Silver, Neil Spencer, Joop Visser and Cliff White.

An extra tip of the shades to:
Matthew Evans, Walter Donohue, Pete Townshend, Tony Wadsworth, Mike Heatley. Not forgetting Bob Willoughby for his truly wonderful cover shot of Chet Baker (1953) and Claude Nobs and the staff of the Montreux Jazz Festival – 20 years of inspired excellence.

The Michael Ochs Archives, 45 Breeze Ave, Venice, California, USA 90291.
The Marquee Club/National Jazz Federation Archives, London.
The Mr R&B and Orkester Journalen Archives, Sweden.
The Franco Milano Archives, Italy
The Eden Du Lac Hotel, Montreux, Switzerland.
New Musical Express, Melody Maker, The Wire, Down Beat, *Fabbri Editions,* Ebony, Swing Journal, *The British Film Institute.*
Mole Jazz Records (London), Doug Dobell's Records (London), Ray's Jazz Records (London), Rock On Records (London), Les Mondes du Jazz (Paris), Bleecker Bob's Golden Oldies, Greenwich Village (New York), Howard Rumsey s Concerts By The Sea, Redondo Beach (California).

To the following recording companies for the use of various album sleeves:
A & M, Ace, Blue Note, CBS/Epic, EMI, F-Beat, Fantasy/Contemporary, IMS, Island, MCA, PolyGram, Mr R & B, RCA, WEA.

Thanks Andy for making it look fantabulous.

Colin MacInnes, Absolute Beginners, *Allison & Busby Ltd, 1959*
© *Colin MacInnes Estate 1959*

David Goodis, Down There, *published in* Nightfall, *Zomba Books, 1983*
© *Gold Medal 1956*

David Goodis, Dark Passage, *published in* Nightfall, *Zomba Books, 1983*
© *Saturday Evening Post 1946*

W.R. Burnett, Vanity Row, *published in* Four Novels, *Zomba Books, 1984*
© *W.R. Burnett 1952*

Jack Kerouac, On The Road, *Andre Deutsch, 1958*
© *Andre Deutsch 1958*

Allen Ginsberg, Howl, *from* Collected Poems 1947-1980, *Harper & Row, Publishers, Inc, 1980*
© *Allen Ginsberg 1955*
Reprinted by permission of Harper & Row, Publishers, Inc.

Beware Brother Beware *recorded by Louis Jordan (MCA) (Lasca, Moore, Adams)* © *Anglo-Pic Music*

Friendship *recorded by Louis Jordan (MCA) (Demetrius, Jordan)* © *Preview Music*

I'm Gonna Move To The Outskirts Of Town *recorded by Louis Jordan (MCA) (Weldon, Jacobs)* © *Leeds Music*

PICTURE CREDITS

2) Mr R&B 5) Melody Maker 13) RC Collection 15) Marquee/NJF 17) Marquee/NJF 21) Slim Gaillard 22) RC Collection 23) Orkester Journalen 24) RC Collection/Prestige-Fantasy 26) Marquee/NJF 28) Michael Ochs, Bullmoose Jackson, RC Collection 30) Orkester Journalen, Michael Ochs 33) Orkester Journalen 34) Franco Milano, Ace Records, Marquee/NJF 37) Charly Records 38) Mr R&B 45) RC Collection 46) Michael Ochs, 47) RC Collection 48) Mr R&B 49) EMI 51) RC Collection, Marquee/NJF 53) RC Collection 54-55) Michael Ochs 57) Michael Ochs 63) Fantasy Records 67) Gretch Drums 68) Franco Milano 68) RC Collection 69) RC Collection 71) RC Collection 73) Bob Willoughby 77) Fantasy/Contemporary Records, Ted Hallock, Franco Milano 79) Bob Willoughby 81) Fabbri 83) Gretch Drums 111) RC Collection 125) Bleddyn Butcher 129) Pennie Smith 137) CBS Records 140) Chuck Berry Frank Driggs Collection 142) RC Collection

Our gratitude to Columbia/Warner/EMI, 20th Century Fox, Universal, MCA, Paramount, MGM for their assistance in tracing original material.

A soundtrack to acccompany this book is available on EMI Records.